COLLABORATIVE INQUIRY IN PRACTICE

COLLABORATIVE INQUIRY IN PRACTICE

Action, Reflection,
and Meaning Making

John N. Bray • Joyce Lee

Linda L. Smith • Lyle Yorks

Foreword by Elizabeth Kasl

Sage Publications, Inc.
International Educational and Professional Publisher
Thousand Oaks ■ London ■ New Delhi

For information:

Sage Publications, Inc.
2455 Teller Road
Thousand Oaks, California 91320
E-mail: order@sagepub.com

Sage Publications Ltd.
6 Bonhill Street
London EC2A 4PU
United Kingdom

Sage Publications India Pvt. Ltd.
M-32 Market
Greater Kailash I
New Delhi 110 048 India

Printed in the United States of America

Library of Congress Cataloging-in-Publication Data

Collaboratiave inquiry in practice: Action, reflection, and making
    meaning / by John N. Bray . . . [et al.].
        p. cm.
    Includes bibliographical references and index.
    ISBN 0-7619-0646-0 (cloth: acid-free paper) — ISBN 0-7619-0647-9 (pbk.:
acid-free paper)
    1. Social sciences—Research. 2. Group work in research. I. Bray,
John N. II. Title.
H62 .C5657 2000
300'.7'2—dc21
                                                                        00-008152

            02   03   04   05   06   7   6   5   4   3   2

Acquiring Editors: Peter Labella/C. Deborah Laughton
Editorial Assistant: Eileen Carr
Production Editor: Diana E. Axelsen
Editorial Assistant: Cindy Bear
Typesetter: Tina Hill
Indexer: Mary Mortensen
Cover Designer: Michelle Lee

Contents

Foreword

From my personal experience, I appreciate the value of this book. Since 1993, I have been teaching health and human service professionals, educators, human resource managers, and community organizers how to use collaborative inquiry. The questions that I am asked most frequently are the questions that are answered in these pages. In fact, I have shared early drafts of this book with practitioners and heard their "rave reviews" of its practical guidance.

The authors of this book began their work as novice collaborative inquirers when they were doctoral students in the Adult Education Guided Independent Study (AEGIS) program at Columbia University's Teachers College. I feel privileged to have served as faculty advisor for the remarkable dissertation project they designed to study collaborative inquiry as a learning experience. As part of their project design, they decided each of them would initiate and participate in an inquiry project. They soon discovered that they could find scant practical guidance for either getting started or proceeding with facilitation of the collaborative inquiry process.

This book responds to their felt need. It captures practical knowledge the authors have developed, from initial experiences during their dissertation work and from their ongoing practice as adult educators who have continued to facilitate adult learning through collaborative inquiry. Based on systematic analysis of their own experience, the authors identify a broad array of often-posed questions and offer insights that can

provide new inquirers with a sense of confidence about what to anticipate and how to proceed.

This book fills a special niche. Currently, there are three books that
provide valuable insights about this process. Peter Reason (1988b,
1994b) has edited two volumes of case studies; John Heron (1996) has
written a definitive theoretical discussion distilled from wisdom gained
during 25 years of reflective practice. I use all three of these books in my
teaching and deeply appreciate their merits. Much as I appreciate their
value, I also know from my experience as a teacher what is lacking. Case
studies provide the reader with access to many different experiences
with the inquiry method, but they tend to focus on the topic of the
inquiry, not its processes. Thus, the reader who comes with questions about process must search "between the lines" for answers. John
Heron's book is truly extraordinary. My colleagues and I value his work
for its brilliant analyses of participatory epistemology. As a practitioner
gains experience, this is a book to which he or she can turn for theoretical insight. However, I believe that it is difficult to appreciate the richness of Heron's contribution until one has acquired some personal
experience to use as context.

Although the authors of this book cannot substitute for experience,
they offer the next best thing—lots of concrete examples drawn from
their combined practice of collaborative inquiry. To the reader who is
not new to the collaborative inquiry process, I believe you will find
affirmation of your own experience in these pages and possibly new
insights. To the reader who is new to collaborative inquiry, I say with
confidence that when you participate in your first inquiry, you will be
embarking on a learning adventure with potential for being among your
most energizing and significant learning experiences.

Although there is no substitute for your own experience, I entice you
on your way by offering you a collage of experience—painted when the
authors were engaging in their own first inquiries and lovingly assembled by me.

> I am not sure why I want to take the cooperative inquiry option. . . . All things
> considered, [a different option] is the rational choice. . . . I don't need any
> extra work, I should pursue the topic which will fit more easily into my other
> work. . . . Yet the ideas of cooperative inquiry are . . . compelling to me, I
> can't let it go. On the other hand some of it seems a little crazy. . . . (Yorks,
> 1995, p. 77)

If you find
strawberries in crystal snow,
will you run away?
(Zelman, 1995, p. 91)

I dreamed a wonderful dream that left me full of peace. . . . The dream was
about CI [collaborative inquiry] . . . I was running towards a very deep can-
yon and I could not see the valley floor . . . then like magic a clear, large bal-
loon appeared. It drifted into my hands and I knew that I could toss it to my
CI buddies on the other side. When I did so, it came back iridescent and
more brilliant . . . (Smith, 1995, p. 260)

There is power that
derives from friends who listen
to your deep heart's core.
(Zelman, 1995, p. 258)

Today, I tried to give my dissertation buddies my mind map of what happened in our dorm meeting session. The response was "it didn't make sense"
and I feel sad. (Smith, 1995, p. 261)

Sometimes, an individual whose meaning is not resonating with the group
will decide to "let go." How one decides to let go of a particular perspective
is a complicated process. We have learned to "let go" because we came to
realize that letting go is not "giving up.". . . We have learned that if an idea is
important, it will come around again after our discussions have created a
perspective that makes its importance clear to all of us. An important factor
in helping us learn to let go is the lack of ego posturing in our group. (Group
for Collaborative Inquiry & thINQ, 1994, p. 62)

The First Canto [from "Strapped to the Wheel"]
Strapped to the wheel,
what a peculiar cart!
Each must move
for all to advance.
If I am I,
how can I be us?
In being we,
am I not me?
Strapped to the wheel
on a road so uneven,

a solitary bump, one and five perceptions.
Start, stop, turn, reverse,
all then one,
one then all.
Five wheels, one cart,
five journeys, limitless journeys.
    (Bray, 1995, pp. 255-256)

In this flirtatious
dance, I am a part of you . . .
I keep my distance.
    (Zelman, 1995, p. 250)

Streams of Meaning
Bubbling up from our beings
Streams of inquiry coalesce
Beckoned by a single question
Only wanderers will solve.
We assembled, five testers of waters,
Apprentice stream searchers
Seekers of wisdom
Of truth and utility
Canteen carriers in the wide wading pool . . .
Streams of inquiry
Become streams of meaning
Gather momentum and speed along.
Rivulets of knowing
Crack frozen lakes within us
Melt icy patches,
Thaw out our minds.
Mists of myopia
Make heavy our hearts
Humidify our souls.
They meander in serpentine fashion
Through personal geographies
Through professional topographies
Rocks of habit erode from the flow . . .
    (Gerdau, 1995, pp. 356-357)

Assumptions attacked,
I can fasten myself to
a rock, or transform.
    (Zelman, 1995, p. 262)

Roller Coaster
To see what it was like,
they ventured on the coaster.
What an odd group of venturers.
Powered to the top,
by the hamsters in their wheels.
None had known what the ride would be.
Some believed that in their intellect
the ride would find meaning.
But as the train crested that designed rise,
they realized the ride would be more.
Yelling, screaming, vitalized
they careened down the slope.
Being thrown for a loop
drained their energy.
Outside and inside the car,
they hurtled on.
Some thoughts went back to why,
others looked only at the second.
All else had departed their minds
in the rush that enveloped them.
Some clung fiercely to each other,
some rode by themselves.
Eventually the end was in sight,
eventually they stopped.
They asked if they could ride again.
In the days since that ride
some have said that it started at the crest,
others say it started at the ticket booth.
Having ridden the coaster,
they are no longer what they once were.
    (Bray, 1995, pp. 137-138)

Participants in this group need to have an eagerness to experiment and a very
high tolerance for ambiguity. (Yorks, 1995, pp. 1-2)

Ours has been a good conversation. (Yorks, 1995, p. 346)

To the authors of this book, I repeat my often-spoken gratitude for all
that I learned and am still learning from our journey together. I draw
continually on the knowledge you created and shared with me. My heart
sings when I think of all that you added when you came forward in

response to my invitation seeking students "eager to experiment and able to tolerate ambiguity." I salute your creativity, integrity, critical thinking, unfailing discipline and determination, playfulness, humor, patience, unquenchable curiosity, and of course, grand capacity for experiment and ambiguity.

—Elizabeth Kasl
California Institute of Integral Studies
San Franciso, California

Acknowledgments

First and foremost, we have to thank all our co-inquirers in the various collaborative inquiry groups we have been associated with. Without them, this book would not exist. We also need to acknowledge the time and energy of Matthias Finger, Maxine Greene, Kathleen Loughlin, Peter Reason, and William Torbert, each of whom went out of their way to offer various kinds of expertise during our dissertation work. Special thanks are due to Victoria Marsick who, as department chair, provided critical support to what was a very radical and potentially controversial dissertation project. Without the contributions of each of these scholars and educators, we would not be doing the work we are doing today. They, of course, bear no responsibility for ideas and arguments expressed below. We also thank Peter Labella at Sage for his helpful feedback and support throughout this project, and C. Deborah Laughton for bringing it to completion.

No expression of thanks is adequate for the role Elizabeth Kasl has played and continues to play in our professional lives. She has been a mentor, colleague, and, most important, a friend. Her scholarship and work with students are characterized by intellectual courage, high personal integrity, and seemingly tireless energy. We have often marveled at her dedication and reaffirmed among ourselves how much we value her as a friend. She personifies the ideals of living the learning and collaborative inquiry.

We thank the following reviewers for their suggestions: Allan Bordow, Anne F. Eisenberg, Michelle Golden, Martha L. P. MacLeod, and Karen Norum.

Introduction

In the fall of 1991, five doctoral students at Teachers College responded to an invitation from Elizabeth Kasl to investigate the possibility of participating in a very unusual dissertation experience. In June, Elizabeth had issued an invitation expressing her interest in working with a small group of students who might be willing to participate in a process of collaborative inquiry, exploring how new paradigm research contributes to adult learning. In her remarks, she tempered her invitation with the caution that the project would require the participants to be able to "tolerate ambiguity." Apart from learning more about collaborative inquiry as both a research and adult learning strategy, she had no particular design in mind. That would emerge from the students, if any, who responded to her proposal.

In September 1991, the five of us—John Bray, Joyce Gerdau (now Lee[1]), Linda Smith, Lyle Yorks, and Annette Zelman—embarked on a journey into collaborative inquiry, pursuing our own inquiry question into how learning is experienced in CI. In addition to our inquiry together, we each initiated other collaborative inquiry groups in our practice areas, pursuing questions of our own. As the reader will soon discover, we were a diverse group in terms of areas of professional practice, prior experience and training, and learning styles. John was a high school science teacher and staff development specialist in upstate New York. Joyce was a consultant with a professional development agency in

New Jersey specializing in integrating technology into school curricula. Linda was a consultant in Washington, D.C., working in the area of community development and helping not-for-profit agencies. Lyle was a professor of management at a state university in Connecticut where he was coordinating a master's program. Annette was an administrator at a large community college near New York City. During the course of our journey, we not only learned about our inquiry questions and the process of conducting this kind of inquiry, but also explored the philosophical and theoretical issues that provide justification for its practice. We adopted the name thINQ (for the Inquiry) as a group name for our reporting our learning in the public arena. Upon completion of this experience and our work together in 1995, most of us have continued to work with this form of inquiry in our professional practices as adult educators and researchers, in school systems, community organizations, and other educational settings.

We are not reporting on these experiences here, although they are the basis for this book. Such reports are available elsewhere (Bray, 1995; Gerdau, 1995; Group for Collaborative Inquiry and thINQ, 1994; Smith, 1995; thINQ, 1993, 1994; Yorks, 1995; Zelman, 1995). Here we share our experience in the initiation and conduct of collaborative inquiry. This book is the product of a collective writing project about collaborative inquiry, drawing on our experience in various inquiries.[2]

There is a certain paradox involved in writing about methods for conducting CI. As a practice of inquiry, it resists much conventional thinking about how research should be practiced. On the other hand, we have become aware of the need for sharing ideas and experience about forms of CI practice if this form of human inquiry is to advance. Our goal here is to provide a framework for those interested in initiating this kind of inquiry as both a method of research and a way of structuring adult learning experiences.

We write with the provision that we understand our task to be one of furthering the dialogue about collaborative inquiry and with no intent of arguing for an orthodox way of practicing CI. For while collaborative inquiry is a very fluid and experiential form of human inquiry, it is also a very rigorous one with its own concerns about the validity of the learning that emerges. We believe that it is through open discussion of methods that CI will continue to develop, spread in its application, and continue to contribute to social, group, and individual learning and development.

ORGANIZATION OF THE BOOK

Chapter 1 provides an introduction to the concept of collaborative inquiry as we practice it, contextualizing our experience in the literature that has provided the foundation for our work. To help orient the reader, brief summaries of our five field groups are also provided. We provide a definition of collaborative inquiry and a map for understanding its fluid process.

Chapter 2 contains an introduction to the key ideas from pragmatism and phenomenological traditions, which will situate collaborative inquiry for the reader. Chapter 3 examines collaborative inquiry in the context of other action-oriented methods of inquiry, some of which are clearly helping to advance the emerging new paradigm of inquiry, while others are arguing for a legitimate place for themselves within the traditional one. Readers who are familiar with participatory human inquiry and are seeking ideas for implementing collaborative inquiry may wish to skim or even skip this material and proceed to Chapter 4. The same can be done by readers who are engaging in this kind of inquiry for the first time as participants and are seeking to gain a better understanding of the process from a practice perspective. For students and others in an academic setting, however, Chapters 2 and 3 provide a context for understanding the learning theory and nuances of this approach to inquiry.

Chapters 4 through 6 elaborate the process of conducting a collaborative inquiry. These chapters meet the fundamental purpose of this book—providing direction for the practice of collaborative inquiry. Chapter 7 raises some issues for future development of this methodology.

AN INVITATION TO INQUIRY AND DIALOGUE

This book is an invitation, a direct descendent of the invitation we received from Elizabeth almost a decade ago. The invitation is for others to experiment with collaborative inquiry, to pursue significant and compelling questions that are not being adequately addressed and responded to through other forms of inquiry, and to contribute themselves to the dialogue.

Four of us—John, Joyce, Linda, and Lyle—have participated in the completion of this book. Annette chose not to pursue the project. She has, however, been an important part of our experience of learning, and our thinking has been influenced by her in many ways. We have missed her in this project.

NOTE

1. Joyce Gerdau has married and has taken the name Lee.
2. Authors are listed alphabetically and the listing does not imply order of authorship.

1

Collaborative Inquiry: A Paradigm for Adult Learning Through Research

A group of community women working as peer counselors to promote breastfeeding in the sixth largest Spanish-speaking center in the United States meet for three years to inquire into ways they can lower the barriers to peer counseling (Smith, 1995). A group of faculty and administrative staff on a community college campus in New York State explore the question "How can we promote intuition?" They interchangeably use the words "promote," "foster," and "nurture" to explore and nurture intuition in themselves, while examining the use of intuition in the classroom (Zelman, 1995). Nine professional development specialists from a division of the State Department of Education in New Jersey inquire into how educators can be assisted to integrate technology into the teaching and learning process (Gerdau, 1995).

Each of these groups came together to participate in a very powerful method for conducting human inquiry and facilitating adult learning—collaborative inquiry (CI). At the conclusion of their time together, each group had collectively construed from their lived experience new meaning about their world—meaning that, through repeated cycles of reflection and action, they found to represent valid knowledge and to have a significant influence on their practice.

This book is intended as both an invitation and an initial guide for people interested in pursuing an imaginative and a holistic approach to human inquiry. Our belief about the power of collaborative inquiry is

---

AUTHORS' NOTE: Throughout this volume, the names John, Joyce, Linda, and Lyle refer to the authors of this book: John Bray, Joyce Lee, Linda Smith, and Lyle Yorks.

based on our own lived experiences, including participation in collaborative inquiries with varied groups (thINQ, 1994). We also draw on the growing number of reports from others using variations of this approach (Group for Collaborative Inquiry, 1991; Group for Collaborative Inquiry & thINQ, 1994; Reason, 1994b).

Our initial experience with collaborative inquiry was as members of a group formed at Teachers College, Columbia University, for the purpose of pursuing dissertation research into CI as a method for fostering adult learning. In addition to this "core group," each of us initiated and participated in another "field group" in our various areas of professional practice. (Summaries of these field inquiries are presented at the end of this chapter, in Box 1.1. It provides an introduction to our work to give the reader a context for many of the examples in the book.) Combined with our own inquiry, all six groups provided a federated design offering a powerful window into the dynamics of collaborative inquiry. This intensive 3-year experience demonstrated for us the power of this methodology as a vehicle for both research and adult learning. Subsequent to this experience, as individuals we have been involved in various additional collaborative inquiry groups in school settings, in not-for-profit agencies, in universities, and in community settings. (One of these other inquiries is summarized in Box 6.1 at the end of Chapter 6; two others are described in text in Chapter 7.) We have found that CI makes systematic human inquiry accessible to people in a truly participative and democratic way. As such, it is a significant tool for adult educators and others seeking to facilitate learning that helps people make meaning from their lived experience, and to foster change in their lives. In addition, collaborative inquiry can produce meaningful knowledge for the public arena—working collaboratively for the purpose of constructing knowledge and theory for public discourse (Group for Collaborative Inquiry & thINQ, 1994).

COLLABORATIVE INQUIRY: A METHOD FOR CONDUCTING PARTICIPATORY RESEARCH AND FACILITATING ADULT LEARNING THROUGH EXPERIENCE

Collaborative inquiry is one of several participatory, action-based inquiry methods that have emerged as innovative ways of improving practice and developing new knowledge, especially in the fields of education, community development, and organizational studies (Brooks & Watkins, 1994). Other action inquiry methods closely related to collaborative inquiry are participatory action research, action science, and appreciative inquiry. The relationship of these methods to collaborative inquiry is the focus of Chapter 3.

Partially derived from the tradition of action research, collaborative inquiry is, nevertheless, a radical departure from it. Inspired by John Heron's (1981, 1985, 1988) ideas about cooperative inquiry and Peter Reason's and John Rowan's work (Reason, 1988b; Reason & Rowan, 1981a) on participatory human inquiry, CI rests on an evolving paradigm of inquiry that celebrates participation and democracy in the research process. These two characteristics are seen as essential for meaningful inquiry into the dilemmas, questions, and problems that are part of the human condition.

Collaborative inquiry also assumes that understanding and improving the human condition requires an approach that honors a holistic perspective on what constitutes valid knowledge. Effective collaborative inquiry demystifies research and treats it as a form of learning that should be accessible by everyone interested in gaining a better understanding of his or her world. Contributing to the realization of this potential for democratizing human inquiry as an adult learning practice is a primary purpose of this book.

The practice of collaborative inquiry as described in this book has its roots in *Human Inquiry,* a seminal volume edited by Peter Reason and John Rowan (1981a). Drawing on the work of researchers in a variety of academic fields around the world, the new paradigm research described in *Human Inquiry* covers a broad spectrum of participative research practices, reflecting an eclectic approach to inquiry. Common to all forms of participatory human inquiry is the tenet of working collaboratively with subjects and avoiding a manipulative, elitist approach to the research enterprise. Also common to all these research practices is developing knowledge in field settings as a catalyst for change—personal change, organizational change, and large-scale social change. Producing change is an important test of the validity of the knowledge derived through collaborative inquiry (P. Reason, personal communication, 1992). Participation in the design and conduct of inquiry and reflecting on experience obtained through taking action on the inquiry question are the two defining ideas of participatory human inquiry.

Cooperative Inquiry

Our interest in this kind of inquiry was stimulated by the model of cooperative inquiry developed by John Heron (1981, 1985, 1988) and elaborated by Peter Reason (1988a). Heron (1996) has further developed the idea of two or more people conducting human inquiry through a series of cycles in which they alternate between having experience and reflecting together on this experience. His approach rests in part on a belief, arrived at through his own experience with phenomenology, that certain aspects of the human experience cannot be understood by conducting experiments and collecting data from other people. Rather, one must be authentically inside the experience to properly explore and understand it. His early work with phenomenology was the experience of the human gaze—the meaning of experiencing this intense human connection. The work of the aforementioned group on intuition (Zelman, 1995) provides another example of an inquiry in which being inside the experience is the most authentic way of exploring and understanding it.

Heron (1996) extends this idea of the investigator having authentic experience to argue that proper research into social and behavioral experience can be conducted only when the participants are fully engaged as self-directing persons. Many behavioral scientists engaged in action-oriented research have struggled with the conflict between their traditional experimental logic, which places subjects in a setting that requires them to behave according to a unilaterally imposed protocol, and the democratic values of the researcher. Chris Argyris (1968) raised this issue many years ago when he questioned the validity of knowledge produced in manipulative settings. Cooperative inquiry turns this dilemma on its head. Heron argues that behavior produced by imposed research protocols tells us nothing about real "personhood" since by definition the subjects are not present as fully self-determining persons. They are subjects acquiescing to the research design.

Consistent with the tenets of hermeneutic phenomenology, Heron maintains that, try as they might, researchers are not able to get outside of their human condition; they can learn only through their own embodiment of it. This learning requires utilizing the full range of a researcher's sensibilities in dialogical relation with other co-inquirers. Propositions about human experience are of questionable validity if they are not grounded in the researcher's own experience. In other words, interpretations obtained by a detached observer through interviews about the experience of others are less likely to convey that experience with the same richness and validity than interpretations arrived at through dialogue on shared lived experience. In the latter collaborative process, the meaning of experience is derived from the inside out, rather than being imposed on experience.

There is a political dimension to Heron's thinking that maintains that people have a right to participate in and express their own values in the design of an inquiry into their experience. Only when this condition holds can researchers ensure that their work empowers, rather than disempowers, participants. Apart from the question of enhancing the validity of the knowledge produced, this is an issue of human rights.

It was Heron's ideas, elaborated by Peter Reason and others (Reason, 1988b), that first attracted us to collaborative inquiry. As adult educators committed to democratic values and the fostering of both transformative learning and valid, useful knowledge, we were intrigued by the idea of exploring a method of inquiry authentically embracing these values. Although each of us had our own individual motives and interests, these broader ideals were a unifying foundation for our involvement.

Collaborative Inquiry

The practice of participatory human inquiry is marked by various strategies distinct in nuance and focus, united in their broad values. We adopted the term *collaborative inquiry,* an umbrella term often used to characterize new paradigm research, to describe our work in this area, primarily to avoid any confusion that we were claiming to be strictly following a particular set of precepts. Being new to this kind of inquiry, we were timid in terms of how our venture might unfold.

One of the tenets of cooperative inquiry is that, although there are parameters that define its practice, there is no dogmatic way to conduct a cooperative inquiry. We understood that, and in fact we found ourselves having to invent our methods as we went along. However, we were initially engaged in this enterprise as part of a doctoral program at Teachers College, Columbia University, a very traditional academic institution. We were already "pushing the envelope" by engaging in our project, and we were concerned about questions from others as to whether we had accurately followed a particular model of inquiry. Adopting the term *collaborative inquiry* provided us with more flexibility to develop our projects with those with whom we were collaboratively engaging in inquiry, without worrying about this constraint. As we extended this method to other applications, we continued to use this term to denote our practice of a form of participative human inquiry, closely aligned with Heron's vision of cooperative inquiry, but not necessarily synonymous with it.

The word *collaboration* carries certain advantages (and a certain amount of baggage). Collaboration suggests a certain degree of tension that we have found to be part of the "meaning-making" process. People wrestle with the divergence that emerges from the different lived experiences they bring to the inquiry process—tension that is mediated by varying learning styles and rooted in different situated interests. Collaborators can engage in inquiry together for divergent reasons and can hold somewhat divergent assumptions about what constitutes knowledge, as long as they agree to the essentials. These essentials are the need to engage in a process of collaborative discovery marked by democratic participation in all phases of the inquiry process, authentic reflection on the interests that motivate their participation, and the honoring of a holistic perspective on the construction of valid knowledge.

The term *collaboration* also carries the semantic baggage of those who collaborated with the powers of hegemony and domination during darker periods of human history. In this sense, "collaborative" serves as a reminder for the need for continuing reflection on the multiple meanings of language and the realities these meanings represent. It also highlights the importance of reflecting on a question raised by Heron (1996, pp. 30-31): In whose interests are we conducting inquiry? Or put another way, with whom are we really collaborating in arriving at our conclusions?

Collaborative inquiry as we practice it finds philosophical support from both pragmatism and phenomenology. It is a logical extension of humanistic psychology and provides a means for fostering transformative learning. In the remainder of this chapter, we first define collaborative inquiry and then introduce a map for understanding its fluid process. This map provides the framework around which the main body of this book (Chapters 4 through 6) is organized.

COLLABORATIVE INQUIRY DEFINED

Collaborative inquiry is a process consisting of repeated episodes of reflection and action through which a group of peers strives to answer a question of importance to them. There are three parts to this definition:

the repeated episodes of reflection and action, the notion of a group of inquirers who are truly peers, and the inquiry question. We turn first to the notion of peers.

Peers as Co-Researchers

Implied in this definition is the assumption that human inquiry is best carried out when the line between researcher and subject is eliminated and all of those involved are full participants in the design, conduct, and communication of the inquiry. Indeed, the notion of co-inquiry—doing research *with* people, rather than *on* them, is the defining principle of collaborative inquiry (Heron, 1996; Reason, 1988a). Elizabeth Kasl, a professor of adult education and a pioneer of collaborative inquiry, observes, "It has been my experience that it's a very hard concept to get. Collaborative inquiry is research based in personal experience, not like an action research team that goes out to collect data from someone else" (E. Kasl, personal communication, October 1996).

What does it mean to engage in inquiry with people rather than on them? Each participant is a co-inquirer—shaping the question, designing the inquiry process, and participating in the experience of exploring the inquiry question, making and communicating meaning. Simultaneously, each participant is a co-subject—drawing on personal experience from inside and outside of the inquiry group to provide a collective pool of experience and insight for analysis and creating meaning. These practices rest on the belief that when researchers engage in the experience under investigation, the result is a more valid understanding of the experience. Issues of power and control, as well as ethics, equally underlie this posture on how human inquiry should be conducted.

This is in stark contrast to traditional experimental, survey, and field research that is widely practiced in behavioral and social science and holds to a strict separation between researcher and subject. In this traditional form of research, professional researchers define the question or problem, determine the methods to be utilized and other design issues, interpret the data, and communicate their conclusions. In short, the researchers, and not their subjects, participate in everything about the research except the experience of the inquiry itself. They do research *on* people.

Heron (1996) sharpens this point about doing research with people by further differentiating from doing research *about* people. He views doing research about people as typical of much traditional qualitative research in which the researcher controls decisions about the research design and partially participates in the experience through forms of participant observation and eliciting comments and perspectives from "subjects" in the field or natural setting. Conversely, the subjects are participating fully in the experience. Some of them may partially participate in decisions about the research, primarily through negotiations with the researcher about the conditions of access to the field setting. Selected "informants" may provide insights or periodic feedback to the researcher, especially as the researcher seeks to establish through "member checks" (Guba & Lincoln, 1981; Miles & Huberman, 1984) the validity of his or her interpretations of what has been seen and heard.

This kind of researcher/subject relationship is typical of much interpretative social science such as ethnography, case study, and grounded theory research. Although the goal of the researcher is to understand the experience of others, the norm of objectivity governs. "Going native" is frowned upon. Heron (1996) characterizes this type of research as "a halfway house between exclusive, controlling research *on* people and fully participatory research *with* people" (p. 27)

Cycles of Reflection and Action on Lived Experience

Reflection on action has long been established as an important element in learning from experience. David Kolb (1984), drawing on Dewey and the pragmatist tradition, has written what many consider the seminal work on learning styles. His model depicts learning as a cycle involving reflection on experience, devising conceptual meaning schema from this reflection, engaging in active experimentation based on this schema, leading to new experience.

Both Jarvis (1992) and Mezirow (1991) have elaborated on the role of reflection in learning. Jarvis has advanced a more differentiated model of learning derived from his research into the Kolb model. He differentiates between three categories of learning responses to experience: (a) nonlearning, (b) nonreflective learning (such as memorization and rote skill learning), and (c) reflective learning. Jarvis further distinguishes among three forms of reflective learning: (a) contemplation, (b) reflective skill learning, and (c) experimental learning. The latter involves trying theory out in practice; the result is new knowledge. Although his description of reflective learning can obviously encompass traditional scientific methods, Jarvis (1992) is describing a more general learning process through which individuals "are always experimenting on their environment and acquiring new knowledge from it" (p. 78). This characterization of reflective learning is consistent with and supportive of collaborative inquiry as a model for facilitating adult learning. His model presents different paths of learning and a more interactive, systemic relationship between practice, experimentation, reflection, and evaluation than Kolb's model.

Mezirow (1991) also asserts a more complex interactive relationship between action and reflection than found in Kolb's work. He writes that "although reflection and action are dialectic in their relationship, they should not be polarized as in Kolb" (p. 6). For Mezirow, reflection is itself a form of action, albeit action that is essentially cognitive rather than overtly behavioral in its manifestation.

Mezirow points out that one can engage in reflection although taking thoughtful action, even if it involves only a split-second pause to assess what one is doing. He differentiates this from ex post facto reflection—looking back on prior learning, focusing on assumptions about the content of the problem or question, or the process or procedures followed in solving the problem or addressing the question. Mezirow differentiates reflection that challenges the presuppositions of prior learning from simple reflection as critical reflection. "Reflection enables us to correct distortions in our beliefs and errors in problem solving. Critical reflection involves a critique of the presuppositions on which our beliefs have be built" (p. 1). In a similar vein, Cell (1984) has described what he calls reflective interpretation, a process of correcting distortions in one's reasoning, perceptions, and attitudes. What these and many other adult learning theorists (Boud, Keogh, & Walker, 1985a; Candy, 1991) have done during the past decade or so is to clearly establish the role reflection plays in learning.

Reflection tends to be initially thought of by many as a cognitive process. However, as those who practice it can readily attest, critical or interpretive reflection engages more than mental processes. Habermas (1971), whose work in the critical theory tradition of the Frankfurt school has been influential in the work of adult learning theorists such as Jarvis and Mezirow, observes that reflection involves both cognitive and affective processes. Describing the emanicipatory impact of reflection during psychoanalysis, Habermas (1971) notes that the process of making unconscious blocking forces conscious "reveals itself as a process of reflection in that it is not only a process on the cognitive level but also dissolves resistance on the affective level" (p. 229). Boud, Keogh, and Walker (1985b) observe that "the reflective process is a complex one in which both feelings and cognition are closely interrelated and interactive" (p. 11).

The cycles of action and reflection that are the heart of collaborative inquiry reveal this strategy to be a powerful approach to learning from experience and, simultaneously, a valid method of conducting inquiry into the nature of human experience. Heron (1985), in developing his ideas on cooperative inquiry, has described it as "a way of systematically elaborating and refining an experiential learning cycle . . . so it is a cooperative way of learning from individual and shared experience" (p. 128). This is the aspect of collaborative inquiry that we wish to emphasize in this book—the potential of collaborative inquiry as a strategy for adult learning and hence adult education, as well as its legitimacy as a form of research.

How these episodes or cycles of reflection and action are organized depends on the question the group is exploring and the constraints under which the group is functioning. For example, the group of community women mentioned in the introduction to this chapter met monthly for a period of more than a year. In contrast, the group of college faculty and administrators participating in an inquiry into how to get students to take more responsibility for their own learning met nine times during the course of an academic year (October through May). The spacing of their meetings varied somewhat based on the needs of the inquiry.

The form and timing of the reflection and action also vary according to the purpose of the inquiry. For example, in the group on intuition, both action and reflection would often take place during the meetings of the group, as members experimented with experiential exercises to generate intuitive knowing and then reflected on these experiences (Zelman, 1995). Members of the group of university faculty and administrators inquiring into learning would often experiment with various teaching methods based on reflections from previous meetings (Yorks, 1995). These experiences would become grist for future reflection and experimentation. This inquiry ended with the group planning a curriculum innovation as a final action. Members of the technology integration group met six times during the course of the academic year. Reflection occurred during group meetings in which multiple perspectives about the meaning of technology sparked animated dialogue.

A Question of Importance to All of the Inquirers

Rigorous reflection, especially when done in a process of social inter-action with others, can be both exhilarating and painful. Commitment to the process comes from the shared commitment to the inquiry question.

The initiators of the inquiry pose the basic question of interest to them and invite others who potentially share this interest to join them. However, the group as a whole may refine or reshape the question as they explore the possibility of working together. During these discussions, the focus of question quite possibly will shift. Those who do not share a significant interest in the revised question may choose not to join the inquiry.

The phrasing of the question determines the parameters of the inquiry. These parameters include (a) what actions by the participants are required for exploring the question, (b) how the experience of the participants will be captured for subsequent reflection and analysis, (c) what validity checks will be adopted by the group, (d) the number and timing of the cycles of action and reflection, and (e) the duration of the inquiry itself. Decisions about these parameters are flexible and alterable as the inquiry proceeds.

Often the question is modified as the inquirers gain insight into their experience and an enhanced ability to articulate what they are really interested in learning. For example, initially our interest in collaborative inquiry centered on its use as a method for fostering adult learning. We posed the inquiry question "What aspects of collaborative inquiry facilitate or impede adult learning?" This question emerged out of considerable discussion about the nuances of what we were interested in learning and our ability to effectively answer the question.

More than a year and a half later, we recognized a disjuncture between how we were attempting to analyze our data and what we were really trying to understand. The wording of the question was directing us toward a rather conventional process of first engaging in open coding—the development of analysis categories—and then closed coding, placing events in our experience into these discrete categories. This analytical approach did not feel right to us—it would not provide us with what intuitively we wanted to know. With this insight, we reworded our question so that it more accurately stated the phenomenon we wanted to understand: "How is adult learning experienced in collaborative inquiry?" This directed us toward a phenomenological approach that permitted us to understand our experience without disembodying it into distinct categories.

The two basic principles regarding the question are that (a) the inquirers can explore it through their own experience and (b) every member of the inquiry is equal relative to the others in terms of his or her ability to address the question. The first principle means that the members of the inquiry can take action relevant to the question. The ability of each participant to engage in the project guarantees that each has a genuine stake in the inquiry, ensuring that all are fully involved in the process. All members of the group are capable of reflecting on and sharing their experience. Thus, they can add their own experience to exploring the question as well as seeking to listen to and understand the experiences of others. This is one of the key differences between collaborative inquiry and many forms of action research in which the researchers seek to capture data from the experience of other people who are essentially subjects of the research.

There are instances in which a person experienced in CI is asked to initiate an inquiry group but is not in a position to take direct action. This places the inquirer in a compromised situation—what Heron calls a partial form of cooperative inquiry. In these instances, the initiator may be prohibited from taking full action on the question. Options for dealing with this situation are suggested in Chapter 4.

The second principle posits a level playing field (to use a sports metaphor) among the inquirers. In a sense, the question under investigation is an equalizer. Although some in the group may be more knowledgeable about certain issues, all are equal in attempting to investigate the question. In this sense they are peers, despite educational or status differences. Their experience becomes the mechanism for unlocking or resolving issues. Monitoring that this equality exists and is maintained in the group is an important obligation of the members of the group.

The three above points—a group of peers, engaging in repeated cycles of action, and reflection on a question of importance to all of them—are the defining characteristics of a collaborative inquiry group. In Chapters 4 through 6, these characteristics are developed in terms of practice. Here we introduce the basic model that organizes this material.

A FOUR-PHASE MAP OF THE
COLLABORATIVE INQUIRY PROCESS

As previously stated, one of the tenets of collaborative inquiry is that there is no dogma or an orthodox way of conducting one. An inquiry should proceed based on the experience that emerges through the repeated cycles of action and reflection. Methods should be developed that allow the inquirers to effectively pursue their question within the context of their setting.

When initiating inquiries, however, we have found that potential participants often need some idea of how the process might evolve. This is especially critical when initiating inquiries in institutional contexts. Hence the initiator is placed in an interesting dilemma—there is a need to provide a general map of the process and a need to avoid suggesting a fixed structure that defeats the intention of collaborative inquiry. This dilemma has been particularly acute in our own work because we are all interested in collaborative inquiry as a way of providing space within institutional settings in which generative learning can take place. This space is akin to what Torbert (1991) has called a *liberating structure:* "a type of organizing that is productive and educates members toward self-correcting awareness" (Fisher & Torbert, 1995, p. 7). One of the things we found in our early work with CI is that it can provide a liberating structure within institutional settings for people to explore questions normally closed to them (thINQ, 1993).

The need for a map to explain the general process, coupled with the primary purpose of this book, which is to provide a guide for those embarking on collaborative inquiry, resulted in Figure 1.1. Inside the half circles are depicted four major phases that an inquiry is likely to pass through. Beside each phase are listed the major issues, choices or options, and activities that are likely to arise. The shadow following the final phase suggests that a subsequent inquiry effort may emerge out of the findings of the initial one.

The map begins with the initiation process, *Forming a Collaborative Inquiry Group.* Once the group is formed and is under way, one should pay careful attention to *Creating the Conditions for Group Learning.* As the process unfolds, the inquiry centers around *Acting on the Inquiry Question* through the repeated cycles of action and reflection. Finally, the primary focus of the group becomes *Making Meaning by Constructing Knowledge.* It is important to remember that this is a fluid process, not a mechanistic one. The timing of concerns grows out of the

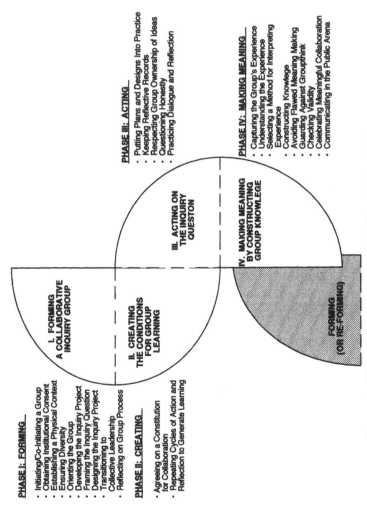

PHASE I: FORMING
- Initiating/Co-Initiating a Group
- Obtaining Institutional Consent
- Establishing a Physical Context
- Ensuring Diversity
- Orienting the Group
- Developing the Inquiry Project
- Framing the Inquiry Question
- Designing the Inquiry Project
- Transitioning to Collective Leadership
- Reflecting on Group Process

PHASE II: CREATING
- Agreeing on a Constitution for Collaboration
- Repeating Cycles of Action and Reflection to Generate Learning

PHASE III: ACTING
- Putting Plans and Designs Into Practice
- Keeping Reflective Records
- Respecting Group Ownership of Ideas
- Questioning Honestly
- Practicing Dialogue and Reflection

PHASE IV: MAKING MEANING
- Capturing the Group's Experience
- Understanding the Experience
- Selecting a Method for Interpreting Experience
- Constructing Knowlege
- Avoiding Flawed Meaning Making
- Guarding Against Groupthink
- Checking Validity
- Celebrating Meaningful Collaboration
- Communicating in the Public Arena

I. FORMING A COLLABORATIVE INQUIRY GROUP

II. CREATING THE CONDITIONS FOR GROUP LEARNING

III. ACTING ON THE INQUIRY QUESTON

IV. MAKING MEANING BY CONSTRUCTING GROUP KNOWLEGE

FORMING (OR RE-FORMING)

Figure 1.1: A Four-Phase Framework of the Collaborative Inquiry Process

inquiry itself. Furthermore, the phases are not necessarily discrete and autonomous. The conditions for group learning can begin during the forming stage, and the process of making meaning and constructing knowledge is woven throughout the process, especially during the cycles of action and reflection that are themselves an important part of the meaning validation process.

This map conceptualizes the process, but does not constrain it. We have found the map to be helpful in communicating to others, and it provides the framework for the main body of this book. The map is offered as a framework for organizing one's thinking about the collaborative inquiry process without reifying it. Chapters 4 through 6 are organized around it. Before this material is presented, however, Chapter 2 provides a brief discussion of some of the intellectual foundations of collaborative inquiry, and Chapter 3 places collaborative inquiry within the broader context of action inquiry methodologies.

BOX 1.1

The Five Field Groups

The Community Women's Group. Linda initiated a collaborative inquiry to learn more about peer learning in a community setting. From years of work with grassroots organizations, Linda believed that collaborative inquiry could capture and formalize the informal learning from community program operations that is often overlooked by community development professionals.

The 11 women who participated in this group had been participating in an outreach program in a suburban area adjacent to Washington, D.C. Members of the group reflected the economic and cultural diversity of the area: four spoke English as a second language; six were women of color; all had family incomes below the median in one of the nation's richest regions.

On a hot, sticky August day, the group met in a church hall furnished with large, overstuffed chairs. Linda came early and posted several large sheets of paper on the wall outlining the concepts of collaborative inquiry. The women arrived, each with an infant, a bundle of toys, and a toddler in tow. They gradually settled in, occasionally becoming distracted by infant needs and toddler demands.

At first, the inquiry process seemed to be a struggle. The outreach leader (who had helped Linda organize the meeting) suggested they try a second session and offered a potluck meal as a part of the program. By the third meeting, the women were using storytelling rounds to shape their inquiry question,

"What are the ways we can lower the barriers to peer counseling?" They were delighted with their question and gave themselves a name, "Becoming Partners."

During each meeting, the women posted their ideas on large sheets of paper to track and reflect upon the peer counseling stories. The stories sparked activity. During the first 6 months of the inquiry, the women took many actions during, and after, their sessions: they surveyed their peers, gave presentations, recorded their journals on audiotapes, wrote poems, developed a funding proposal, set up a 24-hour hotline, and devised a gift basket raffle.

As part of the inquiry, the group reflected on these activities. Each participant learned to describe the value of peer counseling—the group used the common experiences of "mother-to-mother" education, and they learned to recognize their skills as a source of leadership. One member of the group said, "There is power in being able to talk from our experience." Through proposals and presentations, their web of partnerships grew to include the March of Dimes, Georgetown University, and county officials.

The Intuition Group. Annette has long had an interest in how intuition is utilized in teaching and learning. She related her interest to several faculty members and administrators on campus; most were unresponsive, but a few were visibly interested. Four members of the intuition group were recruited in this way; it was as though they had been seeking a forum for exploring intuition all along. Two others joined, creating a group of people engaged in teaching or in facilitating faculty development.

The group had a variety of interests. One member was a poet, another taught psychology, a third taught writing and wrote short stories. A fourth inquirer was an artist and taught art history. Others included a nurse who specialized in Irish culture and a Chinese history scholar turned administrator. Each firmly believed that intuition played a role in her life and in the classroom. They shared the belief that many students were not aware that "educated guesses" were possible and that they could trust knowing that has no words.

The group met in a sublevel room in the library, where others rarely wandered. In the early sessions, the group rejected a number of possibilities for an inquiry question; they met for several sessions without discussing the question's language. Finally, they arrived at the question, "How can we promote intuition?" The word "promote" was later changed to "nurture or foster."

As the sessions developed, the group interpreted the action and reflection aspect of collaborative inquiry in a way different from the other four field groups. Rather than plan actions to take place after each session and reflect on them, the group decided to have in-session exercises and base its reflections on what transpired at each meeting. At the conclusion of their work, the members had a better understanding of nonverbal knowing. They had gained insights into an academic environment that valued arts and literature offered little recognition of the intuitive process involved in their creation. The group, through faculty development workshops, shared its experience with the larger college community.

The Learning Organization Group. Lyle was interested in learning organizations. His work environment was a midsize state university that offered undergraduate and master degrees. To begin the inquiry, Lyle sought the interest and support of a colleague in the sociology department, as well as that of a senior administrator. This sharing of leadership allowed the inquiry to explore co-initiation. The co-initiators approached several members of the college community about the possibility of participating in an inquiry into student learning. Participants in the inquiry included four faculty members representing education, fine arts, management, and sociology, plus two administrators, an associate dean, and a senior academic officer.

There was considerable discussion around the meaning of the words "responsibility" and "learning." Further discussion clarified that the inquiry should extend beyond focusing on the traditional classroom as the only arena of learning. The group agreed to the inquiry question, "How can we get students to take more responsibility for their own learning in a way that makes the university a learning organization?" Universities are in the business of generating learning, and it seemed valuable to explore the learning experiences of students from a systemic view, examining how student culture, curriculum structure, and classroom methods coalesced.

There was tension during the early meetings, in which members spent time discussing classroom experiences and student perspectives. On reflection, it became clear that participants had brought their expectations from campus politics into the meeting room. The unspoken question was "Will this be just another faculty committee?"

During their January session, the group met off-campus, where they experienced a pivotal understanding, found enthusiasm, and began to know each other on a more personal level. They shared experiences and issues that enabled them to establish a high level of trust. This mutual trust was useful to them in their work both inside their inquiry meetings and in other aspects of their professional lives.

In the spring, the group planned a learning community experiment for the upcoming fall semester. They created a cohort of freshman business majors who took four of their five courses together; their faculty met as a team to create learning links among the courses. The courses were Introduction to Sociology, Introduction to the Theatre, Introduction to Management, and College Writing. This experiment was reflected on, evaluated, and modified during the spring semester. The lessons learned were incorporated into a larger faculty process involving the academic advisement center, an organizational learning-system approach. Eventually, a similar design was expanded to include other faculty clusters.

The Teacher Group. John sought more meaningful ways for teachers to learn and develop their practices. He worked in a small public school located in northern New York.

With a teaching load of six 40-minute classes, most involving separate preparations, teachers in the school had little free time to interact with one another as professionals. Using collaborative inquiry, John believed a group of teachers could find a way of helping themselves and improving their practice. John initiated the inquiry by seeking assistance from the school superintendent, who agreed to fund an outside meeting space and to provide substitute teachers for the monthly inquiry sessions.

At the first faculty meeting of the school year, John invited all interested teachers. Eight faculty members accepted his invitation and attended an informational session the following month. As the inquiry meetings progressed, the teachers affirmed each other's contributions and teaching activities. They also changed their question from "How can we improve our practice?" to "How can we improve our practice by creating a sense of community?" As a part of their collaboration, several teachers viewed their work from a changed perspective. One member said that the inquiry "got my juices going again; it got everybody thinking again, and wondering again, and that's the nice part of it." When the teachers had completed the inquiry's goal, they found themselves wanting to do more. The inquiry members continued to share support and exchange ideas informally. Most recently, John received additional funds to develop this inquiry further.

The Technology Group. Joyce sought to investigate the impact of educational technology on teaching and learning. She recruited nine inquirers, who she respected for their knowledge and curiosity. All held educational leadership positions as either administrators, staff developers, or coordinators of programs for the state of New Jersey. With one exception, the participants had no history of working together, but they were united in a desire to understand technology and education.

The group met six times for about 3 hours each during the academic year. Most of the meetings were held in a training room in the agency where Joyce worked, which was located at the convergence of three highways that provided easy commuting.

Through a process of brainstorming and discussion of interests, the group arrived at the question, "How can educators be assisted in planning for and integrating technology into the teaching/learning processes at their respective sites?" By the end of their six sessions, the group formulated useful guidelines for their respective practices. They also came to understand the human dynamics as a part of educational technology.

2

Philosophical Foundations of Collaborative Inquiry

It is not necessary to understand the philosophical basis of collaborative inquiry to participate in one. Most of the participants in the inquiries we have initiated could care less about the philosophy. We dearly want to avoid the trap of intellectualizing a process that has as one of its strengths the ability to demystify and democratize the process of constructing knowledge.

The question then arises—Why address the philosophical issue at all? There are two reasons. First, it is for the readers of this book who are students of adult education and related fields and will both be interested in and find their practice informed by it. We believe that being grounded in a philosophical foundation is an asset to those seeking to determine the extent they may choose to engage in CI as a significant part of their practice. This grounding is especially important for those inquirers who intend to offer their findings for wide dissemination in the public arena—something we encourage as part of the practice of CI. However, doing so is likely to raise questions from others about the basis for their claim to legitimate knowledge. Second, scholars and researchers have a right to know how we place our work in the broader context of philosophy of knowledge as part of the process of assessing it. Those readers who are primarily interested in gaining direction for applying collaborative inquiry in their practice can choose to skim or skip this short chapter, and even the next one, which places CI in the broader context of action-oriented research technologies.

PHILOSOPHICAL PERSPECTIVES OF
LEARNING FROM EXPERIENCE

In Chapter 1, we defined collaborative inquiry as a process consisting of repeated episodes of reflection and action in which a group of peers strives to answer a question of importance to them. Virtually by definition, then, the role experience plays in learning is relevant to understanding the practice of collaborative inquiry. There are two major traditions of western philosophy in which experience plays a central role in terms of learning: (a) American pragmatism and (b) the phenomenological tradition that emerged from European scholars emphasizing the concept of the "life-world."

Dewey's American Pragmatism

The writings of John Dewey made pragmatism a distinctly American philosophy (Elias & Merriam, 1980). Edmund Husserl's transcendental phenomenology extended the neo-Kantian project that was directed toward overcoming the "naïveté of objectivism" (Gadamer, 1993). Both traditions were influenced by the radical empiricism of William James.

In James's radical empiricism, Dewey found the foundation for an original American philosophy that provided a method for using intelligence as an antidote to the unreflective individualism that pervaded American life (McDermott, 1973, p. 41). Pragmatism, for Dewey, was an extension of historical empiricism, but with a fundamental difference—"it does not insist upon antecedent phenomena but upon consequent phenomena; not upon the precedents but upon the possibilities of action" (p. 50). Dewey considered this focus on consequences rather than antecedent phenomena to be revolutionary in its implications. The future, as well as the past, became a source of interest that gave meaning to the present. Individuals, as the carriers of creative thought, were seen as "authors of action" (p. 56) capable of creating the future. In Dewey's pragmatism, the function of intelligence was not just to copy the objects of the environment, but to determine how "more effective and more profitable relations with these objects may be established in the future" (p. 54).

Dewey viewed experience as the *sine qua non* of learning, a function of individuals interacting with their world. For Dewey, human experience is central to arriving at knowledge, and truth is found in the consequences of actions—there are no absolutes. Experience must be understood from both an active and a passive element. Activity was not in itself experience. Only when the changes made through action are reflected upon and involve a change in the person in the form of learning is activity transformed into significant experience.

This reciprocal relationship between action and reflection in transforming activity into meaningful experience, coupled with the validation of experience through the nature of the observable consequences, is inherent in the practice of collaborative inquiry as described here. However, Dewey's thinking about the methodology of carrying out this approach differs significantly.

In Dewey's pragmatism, how people learn from their experience is couched in concepts derived from the scientific method. Darwinism had a strong direct influence on Dewey (1910), as did the empirical methods of the new objective psychology. In education, he called for the controlled type of learning exemplified in science (Elias & Merriam, 1980). For Dewey, reflection meant validity testing in the sense of traditional problem solving (Mezirow, 1991). Dewey's process involved "formulation of the problem, reasoning from evidence, developing hypotheses, testing of hypotheses, and their reformulation based on feedback" (Mezirow, 1991, p. 101). This process of learning from one's experiences provided the basis for growth through lifelong learning.

Dewey provided the basis for the many of the action-oriented inquiry technologies that have contributed to the emergence of new paradigm research and, in some instances, contributed some of the methodologies employed by its practitioners. These include the action research tradition of Kurt Lewin (1946), Rapoport (1970), and Susman & Evered (1978); the Participatory Action Research of Elden (1981), Elden & Levin (1991), Whyte (1991a), and Miller (1994); and the Action Science of Argyris (1982) and Argyris, Putnam, and Smith (1985). The model of experiential learning developed by Kolb (1984) is another product of this tradition. As Heron (1992) notes, the core process depicted by Kolb of reflecting on experience, developing from this reflection a conceptualization of the experience, and testing this conceptualization through subsequent action to produce additional experience for further reflection is an adaptation of the scientific process to everyday experience.

This emphasis on the traditional scientific method with its grounding in objective observation is where collaborative inquiry takes its leave from the tradition of pragmatism in American adult education. As we shall see below, the practice of collaborative inquiry does not necessarily reject the validity of the traditional scientific method for answering certain kinds of questions, but places this method of learning in the broader context of the "life-world." The basis for this position is found in the hermeneutic phenomenology of Hans-Georg Gadamer.

Phenomenology and the Life-World

The phenomenological tradition begins with Husserl (1960), who is generally regarded as the father of phenomenology. Although Dewey built on James's radical empiricism through an emphasis on objectivity, Husserl gave prominence to the role that subjectivity plays in knowing. Gadamer (1993, pp. 245-246) suggests that Husserl's concepts of "horizon" and of "horizon consciousness" were in part suggested by James's idea of "fringes."

Although influenced by empiricism, Husserl's project was directed toward understanding the structures that organized one's consciousness. In pursuing his project, Husserl held that these organizing structures could not "be explained in terms of generalizations 'learned' from experience, but are rather presumed by experience" (Polkinghorne, 1983, p. 41). This pre-given basis for all experience is what Husserl called the life-world.

Husserl did not believe he could replace empiricism as much as enhance it with methods based on the rational tradition. He was striving to develop an objective human science that would be the equivalent of natural science in its objectivity, but with its own methods. It was the application of the methods of the natural sciences to the study of the human condition, not their objectivity, which Husserl rejected.

Phenomenology, like pragmatism, is a topic unto itself. The lineage we are interested in here is hermeneutic phenomenology. It begins with Husserl's student Martin Heidegger and finds its most influential anchors in the philosophical writings of Hans-Georg Gadamer (1987) and Paul Ricoeur (1971, 1974, 1986). Gadamer argues that Husserl's preoccupation with developing an objective human science led him into approaches that are alienated from the actual concept of the life-world that "is the antithesis of all objectivism" (Gadamer, 1993, p. 247).

For Gadamer, the life-world is more fundamental than the empiricism of science because its horizon is the presupposition of all science. We live in the world as historical creatures whose view of the world is pre-given. No matter how much we may strive toward a position above the cultural traditions and the flow of our own history, that position cannot be obtained. Understanding our tradition can occur only within the context of our language, because tradition is itself linguistic in nature. In other words, we are all embedded within a historical tradition that frames our experience of the world and cannot be transcended in its entirely. Language, the medium of communication, is itself part of this frame, or life-world.

This concept of the life-world is basic to Gadamer's understanding of experience. For Gadamer (1993), genuine experience is always negative in the sense that something is experienced as being not what it is supposed to be. Experience inevitably involves many disappointments of one's expectations. "Insight . . . always involves an escape from something that had deceived us and held us captive" (p. 356). Such an experience must become differentiated from the running flow of lived experience that is continually proceeding forward in an irreversible manner. To have an experience requires an act of individual observation (Gadamer, 1993), or attention (Schutz, 1967), that the taken-for-granted is made problematic.

It is here that we find a critical distinction between the project of hermeneutic phenomenology and the pragmatism of Dewey relative to experience and learning. Dewey built his philosophy of pragmatism in large part on the foundation of empiricism. People learn from their experience by applying the scientific method to it. Reflective thinking is triggered by awareness that a problem exists for which there is an uncertain solution. It is largely limited to the interpretation of facts and the application of logical principles (Mezirow, 1991).

From the perspective of hermeneutic phenomenology, learning is an act of interpretation. It involves a fusion of horizons between the horizon of the person (who is immersed in his or her life-world) and the horizon of the lived experience that is the object of attention. This is a dialogic act of interpretation between interpreter and what is interpreted. The outcome is a fusion of horizons from which new meaning emerges. The life-world that is constitutive for the experience is fused with the perspective of the experience.

Beyond the strict tradition of phenomenology, the concept of the life-world is prominent in the critical theory movement of the "Frankfurt School." The most prominent figure from this school in adult learning theory is Jürgen Habermas (1971, 1984). Central to Habermas's theoretical framework is the assumption that through intersubjective communicative competence, human beings can recognize one another as human and shape the course of their affairs. Defining the life-world as "represented by a culturally transmitted and linguistically organized stock of interpretive patterns" (p. 170), he contends that the situations in which people function are very loosely defined in terms of a horizon that shifts with the theme of the interactions and the plan of action involved. As the theme of an interaction shifts, the segment of the life-world relevant to the situation shifts as well. The life-world is always present, but only as the background for an actual scene. Through the medium of language, people simultaneously use and reproduce their life-world.

Through his theory of transformative learning, Mezirow has provided the most direct and prominent introduction of Habermas and the concept of the life-world. His work is part of a growing body of literature on critical approaches to adult learning represented by such figures as Michael Collins (1991), Mechthild Hart (1990), and Michael Welton, (1991), to name but a few. Although each of these writers has a distinct theoretical focus, taken together they provide a penetrating critique of the subtle educative powers of large social structures.

The concept of the life-world provides a comprehensive framing for understanding learning from experience through collaborative inquiry. Collaborative inquiry is a process through which people may find themselves becoming more cognizant of aspects of their life-world. A collaborative inquiry is usually initiated by a person who is uncomfortable with some aspect of their experience and wishes to explore this sense of discomfort. The person joins others with a similar sense of discomfort. In the terms of the present discussion, some aspect of their life-world has been problematized. As they reflect on their lived experience in their inquiry, inconsistencies between the expectations they initially held and their experience as a result of the inquiry become apparent. Aspects of their life-world become even more problematized. As they make meaning from their experience, their personal horizons and the horizons of the life-world under investigation become merged into a new understanding of their world. Usually this new understanding is more comprehensive and more integrated than was their previous understanding, a marker of having experienced transformative learning.

We often had this experience in our own inquiries into how learning is experienced in CI. Early in our experience we struggled with the implications of many of our inquiry methods. Despite having engaged in frequent critiques of conventional research practices, we came to understand that we were not recognizing the full implications of the subject/object split that is a fundamental assumption of the American tradition of pragmatism. For example, as we encountered the boundaryless nature of collaborative inquiry, initially we struggled with the implications of this characteristic of the process. It was difficult to clearly differentiate what learning was "inside" the inquiry and what was "outside" of it. Our experience in collaborative inquiry was influencing our work in other arenas and vice versa. As we explored this quality among ourselves, we came to embrace it as one of the essential themes of the phenomenon. We were learning from being in collaborative inquiry within the context of our world. Many of our assumptions about research were being problematized for us. As we explored these reactions through further reflection and experience, we discovered more and more about our question.

Humanistic Psychology

Humanistic, or third force, psychology emerged from the phenomenological tradition. Maslow, who is widely regarded as the founder of this school, was strongly influenced by existentialism and existential phenomenology. The work of Carl Rogers is perhaps the best example of phenomenological psychology. Rogers (1961) held that a person's behavior is best understood through observation of his or her internal frame of reference. Each individual construes reality in accordance with his or her private world of subjective experience.

Edward Cell (1984), who is heavily influenced by Rogers' writing, is an example of another learning theorist who takes a phenomenological perspective. Immersed in one's life situation, one sees the challenge of developing as a person as that of learning to be significant as a person, having the power to make a difference in one's situation. Doing so requires learning *how* to learn from experience.

The introduction of a humanistic perspective into a field dominated by the mechanistic approaches of behaviorism and experimentalism provided grounding for the theory of personhood. Personhood is a theory based on a wide-ranging phenomenology of human experience that sees the person as a distinct presence in the world (Heron, 1992). Further, the emphasis placed on a holistic approach to psychological inquiry rather than the reductionism of behaviorism and experimentalism, the credibility given to spiritual aspects of life, and the valuing of experientially based knowledge point the way toward the practice of CI as a way of conducting human inquiry. So too is the emphasis given to self-directedness and self-actualization. Even as humanistic psychologists have sought to create a complimentary approach to their more behaviorist colleagues, careful reflection on their writings begs the question of how we can craft a more inclusive, holistic approach to human inquiry. Collaborative inquiry is one possible response to that question.

INNER KNOWING COMPLEMENTING
THE WESTERN MODEL

The eclectic, yet disciplined, integration of the ideas drawn from pragmatism, phenomenology and critical theory, and humanistic psychology provide a context for situating the practice of collaborative inquiry. There are other avenues from which one might arrive at such a practice. We live in a time in which an increasing number of people in the West are experiencing the need to supplement the outwardly focused philosophies of their tradition with the inward focused philosophies of the Eastern cultures. Meditation and spiritual knowing are gaining acceptance as providing a more holistic meaning of the world. Mechanistic metaphors are being replaced by organic ones in our making sense of the world. Masculine and feminine imagery is advanced as being not in conflict but in reciprocal interdependence for co-creation of community. Collaborative inquiry, like other forms of participatory human inquiry, is a vehicle for giving actionable form to these powerful cultural influences.

COLLABORATIVE INQUIRY: SIMULTANEOUSLY
A PROCESS OF ADULT LEARNING AND RESEARCH

In his early work on cooperative inquiry, Heron (1985) described cooperative inquiry as a way of systematically deriving learning from individual and shared experience as people engage in a refined experiential learning cycle. Their advocates commonly position the various forms of participative human inquiry as research processes. We agree that collaborative inquiry is a legitimate form of research and that it is important to maintain this position. To fail to do so is to yield the field on important questions about how human inquiry is commonly conducted—questions that involve issues of power, control, and the validity of knowledge that is imposed on society. Collaborative inquiry is also a way of conducting research into human experience. As such, it is an important methodology for the human sciences.

However, we believe it is also important to emphasize that collaborative inquiry is a process consistent with how people learn. Giving emphasis to this aspect of collaborative inquiry demystifies the process of learning about what it means to be human and inquiring into the questions that confront people in their daily lives. Collaborative inquiry structures a very rigorous process of learning through experience—constructing answers to questions that are highly significant to the inquirers.

Just as collaborative inquiry is a research practice that removes the separation of researcher from subject, so it is a practice of fostering learning that denies that research is a form of learning reserved for specialists. We confronted this issue during our collaborative inquiry into adult learning, in which Elizabeth Kasl, the initiator of our work, commented:

> I don't understand collaborative inquiry as a research process nearly as well as I understand that it's a learning process. And that's probably because of all my traditional biases about what research really is. . . . I was trying to sort out . . . why I want to attach the learning to the making of new knowledge in this context? . . . there could be no finer definition of research than the making of new knowledge. (thINQ transcript, May 1993, pp. 3062-3071)

Validity, or trustworthiness, is central to any learning strategy that claims the mantle of research. In research one has to establish that one's interpretation of experience is somehow valid. This is also the role of critical reflection in adult learning, correcting the distortions in our reasoning and presuppositions (Cell, 1984; Mezirow, 1991). Going through cycles of experience and reflection several times provides for a progressive improvement in "the validity of the reflection by testing it and retesting it against the content of experience and action" (Heron, 1985, p. 129). This, of course, implies the use of methods to enhance the process of validation, methods that will be discussed in later chapters.

ACTION INQUIRY METHODOLOGIES AND COLLABORATIVE INQUIRY

A number of participatory, action-oriented inquiry methods are gradually gaining in popularity among practitioners of adult education and human resource development, and practitioner-focused scholars. These action based inquiry methods include participatory action research, action science, action inquiry, action learning, and appreciative inquiry. Although each of these methods have distinguishing characteristics, they share a focus on praxis—an intense interaction between action and reflection that produces generative learning that changes the life-world of those who engage in it. These methods also bridge the gulf that has emerged between research and practice. Action inquiry strategies are manifestations of growing concerns among some researchers about the usefulness of much contemporary social science. Having presented the intellectual foundations of collaborative inquiry and the defining characteristics of the CI model we turn now to situating collaborative inquiry among this array of action-oriented strategies for learning and inquiry.

3

Collaborative Inquiry and Other Participatory and Action-Based Inquiry Methods

What is distinctive about collaborative inquiry compared to action research or participatory action research? For that matter what are the differences between action research and participatory action research? How does collaborative inquiry differ from action learning? Where, if at all, does action science fit into the practice of collaborative inquiry? These questions are of interest to adult educators, management development specialists, applied behavioral and social scientists, and other practitioners interested in understanding how the field of action-oriented inquiry is evolving.

The answers to these questions are of more than academic interest—they help provide answers to questions important for professional practice. To what extent do competencies and frames of reference transfer from other forms of action-oriented inquiry to CI? How might the experience of practicing collaborative inquiry be different from other forms of practice?

These kinds of questions are not important to all participants in collaborative inquiry. Many participate in CI because it is a way of obtaining answers to troubling or compelling questions. This was certainly the case with the community women and the schoolteachers with whom we have worked. Others, such as some of the technology specialists, had a passing interest in these questions, initially wondering whether CI was, in effect, old wine in new bottles. The university faculty was clearly interested in learning how this method fit with other approaches to learning and inquiry.

As was the case with Chapter 2, this chapter provides a context for CI, honoring its debt to other methods and framing it as one of several action-oriented inquiry methodologies.

ACTION-ORIENTED INQUIRY METHODS: SIMILARITIES AND DIFFERENCES

Action-oriented inquiry is currently enjoying a revival of interest among many scholars and practitioners of adult education, community development, organizational development and management, and other applied behavioral sciences (Brooks & Watkins, 1994). These action inquiry methods make explicit, and celebrate, a basic truism about much human learning—it is essentially a social activity. Traditionally, particularly in America, learning is an individual, competitive experience. Formal schooling is structured so students demonstrate their knowledge in competition with their peers. Likewise, reward systems in academia focus on individual rather than group authorship. Ironically, this individualistic mode contradicts our subsequent work experience in which cooperation and teamwork are vital prerequisites for professional success. The complex problems faced by individuals and organizations today cannot be resolved by one person's heroic efforts; from education to science to business, increasingly, solutions lie in collaborative efforts.

Brooks and Watkins (1994) identify four dimensions that are common to action inquiry strategies. First, their intended result is "the construction of new knowledge on which new forms of action can be based" (p. 11). The second dimension is that those people who comprise the population of a particular research context or setting "should be central to the research process" (p. 11) as active participants in the inquiry process. Third, "the data used in the research process are systematically collected and come from the experience of the participants" (p. 12). The fourth dimension is, as previously mentioned, a focus on generating change in the form of "improvements in professional practice, organizational outcomes, or social democracy" (p. 12).

There are, however, important distinctions among the action inquiry methodologies (Brooks & Watkins, 1994). As we shall see, they vary in their assumptions about knowledge and the relationship of the inquirer to the inquiry question. These assumptions influence the methods used and the extent to which they either mirror or diverge from traditional experimental methodology. Further, depending on how a particular methodology is used, it may serve either the interests of the institutions, the interests of the individuals involved in the inquiry process, or both. The political implications of the inquiry can vary according to whose interests the inquiry serves.

Heron (1996) notes that being clear about whom the research is *for* is as an important concern for cooperative inquiry as the tenet of doing research with, as opposed to *on* or *about,* people. Is the research being conducted for the status and career advancement of an academically based researcher, the enhancement of institutional relationships and prestige, the ability of others to control or in some way maintain dominance over subordinates or students, or for the enhancement and empowerment of each other's lives?

Closely related to the above issue is the extent to which control over the research is shared among everyone involved in the inquiry process and the extent to which control over inquiry design, methodology, interpretations of the data generated, and communication of outcomes is centralized. Finally, action inquiry methods vary in how the learning from the inquiry is intended to be used—contributing to formal knowledge generalizable to many settings or toward solving localized problems that are contextually bounded. The kinds of questions addressed vary from one methodology to another.

The similarities between collaborative inquiry and other action-oriented strategies of research and learning seem evident—the emphasis on reflexivity, taking action, and deriving lessons from the experience. We turn now to some of those strategies and consider the similarities and differences between each and collaborative inquiry.

Action Research

Action research (AR) is in many ways the precursor of all the action inquiry strategies and participatory human inquiry strategies. Because of its foundational influence we will devote considerable attention to it. AR is a cornerstone of the field of organizational development (Burke, 1982), its scholar/practitioners partnering with clients to foster development change in individuals, groups, organizations, and large scale social systems. In addition, it is a popular strategy for educational research.

French and Bell (1995) offer a basic definition of AR as "research on action with the goal of making that action more effective while simultaneously building a body of scientific knowledge" (p. 137). Perhaps the most frequently quoted definition of AR is Rapoport's (1970): "Action research aims to contribute both to the practical concerns of people in an immediate problematic situation and to the goals of social science by joint collaboration within a mutually acceptable ethical framework" (p. 499). Inherent in both of these widely cited definitions is the tension between making a contribution to solving the problems confronting society and the widely accepted criteria of the larger social science community for acceptable empirical research. From the beginning, action researchers have been on the defensive against the larger community of social and behavioral scientists who have challenged the situation-specific nature of their case studies and the often qualitative character of their work.

In 1946 Kurt Lewin introduced the term "action research" as a label for a revolutionary way of conducting social science that linked the generation of theory to changing a social system through action. For Lewin, action research was a means for dealing with social problems, such as racism, through a process of both changing and generating knowledge about the system (Susman and Evered, 1978).

The writings of Lewin soon spawned a movement of action-oriented social scientists, with significant inputs coming from the researchers associated with Tavistock Institute of Human Relations in England in which a set of parallel but independent developments were emerging (Susman & Evered, 1978). The Tavistock model initially drew more on the concepts of the psycho-dynamics of groups (Bion, 1961) and constituted what Trist (1976) has referred to as "a form of field psychiatry" (p. 43). With time, action research became increasingly characterized by systems thinking as a guide for its practice (Emery, 1969; Trist, 1976).

Action researchers embraced the value of being in the field and building knowledge and theory from solutions to "real world problems" (Clark, 1976). Early work in action research represented a significant alternative approach for practicing social science, but continued to be heavily influenced by conventional scientific thinking about the nature of valid knowledge. Clark writes that:

> At the center of action research lies the traditional scientific paradigm of experimental manipulation and observation of effects. . . . But it is field experimentation with a twist: the manipulation or action is introduced, not by the experimenter alone, but by the experimenter in collaboration with the subjects. (p. 1)

For the pioneers of action research, combining discovery with implementation provided opportunities for studying systems as they reacted to experimental interventions. They continued to subscribe to very traditional assumptions about valid scientific knowledge needing to be objectively obtained. An action research team consisted of both researcher(s) and client(s). While decisions about the research process were made in collaboration with the client, the roles were distinct. The client had a practical problem and was assumed to be more interested in learning how to resolve it than in contributing to a formal body of theory. The researcher brought specific skills such as research design, survey development, interviewing, and data analysis. Although interested in helping to resolve the problem, the researcher was also interested in contributing to a more generalized body of theoretical knowledge.

The researcher's skills were applied in a new way, but based on conventional assumptions about the nature of valid knowledge. These assumptions are reflected in the following comment by Deutsch (1968):

> Considerable experience with action research, however, has indicated that the goals of action and the goals of research may often be incompatible. The danger that confronts the research worker in such situations is the possibility that his research design or methodology will be sacrificed to the achievement of the social action objective. (p. 466)

This sentiment is echoed by Seashore (1976) who observed "that there is a degree of inherent incompatibility between action and research" (p. 103). For Seashore, this incompatibility is not absolute and "can be reduced by heightening awareness of design properties, types of scientific contribution, and varieties of valid and useful data" (p. 117). The researcher is charged with making rational choices to optimize both the scientific and the problem-solving outcomes of an action science project.

The theme that emerges throughout this early action research literature is a tension between the demands of taking action in an existing social context and the requirements for establishing valid knowledge in the context of the objectivist paradigm.

As vexing as this dilemma was, another closely related issue was perhaps more so—the relationship between researcher and the subjects of the research. The concept of manipulation, especially as it applied to meeting the prevailing standards of social science research, was troublesome to action researchers who generally held strong values honoring openness and non-manipulation in social relationships. Cherns (1975) makes the point as follows:

> There is an inescapable suggestion of manipulation in the conduct of any action research directed toward organizational change . . . any attempt to obtain "baseline" data for future evaluation involves taking observations for a purpose as yet undisclosed to the participants to avoid the effects of aroused expectancy. The same applies to the use of control groups. . . . Indeed, one sometimes has serious doubts about the whole enterprise of evaluation. . . . [Evaluation] does not allow for the emergent nature of action research objectives. . . . The cautious action researcher knows that a change of objective will ruin the independent evaluation. (pp. 28-29, bracket added)

Action research was seen as more than simply a method for applying social science to real world problems. However conflicted its position, AR began the challenge to the position of the social scientist as a privileged observer and analyst (Clark, 1972).

To summarize, action research was borne out of the motivation to effectively link social science research to the resolution of pressing social problems. This was to be accomplished through collaboration between members of a client system that "held" the problem and trained social scientists committed to helping resolve the problem and making contributions to social science theory. In pursuit of this collaboration, action researchers struggled with forging methods that would produce knowledge that could be justified in academic circles as scientifically valid, while honoring values that moved away from an elitist conceptualization of the researcher role. Over the past several decades the process of developing methods to resolve the dilemmas described above has led to the development of new ways of thinking about research that both solves practical problems and contributes to scientific theory (Elden & Chisholm, 1993). This development has been expressed through a new framing of AR by some researchers as Participatory Action Research (PAR).

Participatory Action Research

Action research has been evolving over the course of the past several decades. The 1960s saw AR suffer something of a setback as the traditional experimental, quantitative approach emerged to dominate the social and behavioral sciences, especially in the United States, with a reemergence of action research occurring during the 1980s. Along with this reemergence came a greater focus on the collaborative dimension of action research practice and a greater emphasis on not only solving problems, but enabling the client system to continue to learn after the researcher leaves the system. Action research efforts became directed toward developing "a higher degree of self-determination and self-development capability" (Elden & Chisholm, 1993, p. 125). This new emphasis introduced the goal of fostering learning how to learn among clients as well as solving problems and generating valid knowledge.

The term "Participatory Action Research" has been adopted by those practitioners of action research who hold this new focus to more clearly set it apart from the elitist assumptions of the traditional, laboratory model of experimental research. Whyte (1991b) has critiqued what he considers the elitist structure of traditional social research:

> The standard model of social research is an elitist or top-down model. It is commonly assumed that, in order to meet the exacting standards of science, the professional researcher should exercise maximum control over the research process, from the initial design to the conclusions and recommendations emerging from the study. . . . Participatory action research challenges this standard model. (p. 272)

In participatory action research the people who participate in the research process become "full partners or co-researchers in running the research process itself" (Elden & Chisholm, 1993, p. 125). This co-participation involves practitioners from the client system in comanaging the entire research process from the research design, through data gathering and analysis to conclusions (Whyte, 1991b). Coupled with the goal of helping the client system to become more self-determining, this coparticipation means that "system members must learn how to make sense of their own data in terms of their own language and in relation to their own perception and values" (Elden & Chisholm, 1993, p. 125). Elden and Chisholm further note that this "New thinking in action research seems to take the social construction of reality seriously. . . . From a constructivist perspective, science can contribute to people realizing their values—envisioning a preferred future and organizing effectively to achieve it" (p. 127). This line of reasoning raises some interesting complexities for PAR researchers who accept the notion of the social construction through collective interaction of an objective reality that is subject to cause-and-effect explanations among participants in a given context. For these researchers, PAR is a research process for those "who want their research to lead to social progress and yet do not want to give up claims to scientific legitimacy" (Whyte, 1991a, p. 8).

This position carries into PAR the tension between being a research process on action with the goal of making action more effective and the need for conforming to the norms of scientific inquiry that remain dominated by traditional models of experimental and quasi-experimental research design. In practice, the movement toward PAR is marked by a wide array of action research practice, accompanied by a diverse set of assumptions about what represents an appropriate warrant for valid knowledge. Historically, action researchers have conceded to their more quantitative and experimentally oriented colleagues that action research is a very elementary and exploratory form of research, valuable either for suggesting lines of more controlled investigation or for adding refinements to general theory produced through statistical research.

Today, many participatory action researchers challenge the notion that the dominant research model is appropriate for answering many questions central to human inquiry and social action. Susman and Evered (1978) summarize the case for a broader warrant for scientific knowledge writing:

> We find that action research is not compatible with the criteria for scientific explanation as established by positivist science. . . . However, in action research, the ultimate sanction is in the perceived functionality of chosen actions to produce desirable consequences for an organization. Action research constitutes a kind of science with a different epistemology that produces a different kind of knowledge, a knowledge which is contingent on the particular situation, and which develops the capacity of members of the organization to solve their own problems. (p. 601)

Elden and Gjersvik (1994), in describing contemporary participatory action research practice in Scandinavian countries, speak of co-generating new knowledge and suggest that they have indications that utilizing participants as co-researchers provides "much more valid data and useful interpretations" (p. 39).

McTaggart (1997a, p. 28) elaborates on the distinction between authentic participation and mere involvement. Authentic participation, he notes, "means sharing in the way research is conceptualized, practiced, and brought to bear on the life-world." It is a responsible agency in both the production of knowledge and the improvement of practice. Citing Tandon's (1988) reference to participants in PAR having control over the whole process, McTaggart notes that authentic participation means that participants may reinterpret and reconstitute the research methodology itself. This emphasis on cogeneration of knowledge moves PAR into the universe of participatory human inquiry.

However, the PAR term itself is shared by two very different groups of researchers. Reason (1994a) identifies two camps of action-oriented researchers who have adopted the label of PAR. One camp, referred to by Reason as the Northern School, is the one described above, a direct descendent of the traditional AR approach. Generally speaking, this school of PAR seeks to reform institutions, striving to make them more democratic.

The second camp, referred to by Reason as the Southern School, openly asserts that knowledge production is inherently a political act. Its goals are liberationist, drawing heavily on the work of Paulo Freire (1970). Practitioners in this liberationist school respond angrily to what they view as a co-optation of their identity, arguing that they originally used this term to describe their work (Reason, 1994a). They further resent the use of the PAR term by action researchers from the traditional school "because this approach is based on a liberal rather than a radical ideology and holds quite different assumptions about the relationship between popular knowledge and 'scientific knowledge'" (p. 328). No doubt use of the same term for very different ways of working with client systems confuses the dialogue among the various forms of participative human inquiry (Brown, 1993; Reason, 1994a; Whyte, 1992). However, McTaggart (1997b) has demonstrated that it is possible to consider PAR in all its manifestations, in an effort to more clearly understand both the differences among various theories and practices of PAR and where and how they converge.

The Relationship of PAR to Collaborative Inquiry

The tradition of action research is in many ways the precursor to the practice of collaborative inquiry. The AR tradition has been instrumental in opening up thinking about alternatives to the dominant experimental model of scientific thinking and has produced a significant subpopulation of social scientists who have challenged, and continue to challenge, the elitist and manipulative practices inherent in this way of conducting social and human inquiry. In the process AR has no doubt created the platform for the broader array of collaboratively structured, action-focused forms of human inquiry that are emerging today. Those practitioners who have moved to the PAR model of co-researcher inquiry are clearly close cousins to practitioners of collaborative inquiry. Some researchers may even move between the two models depending on the context of a particular setting.

Nevertheless, important differences between these two forms of inquiry exist and a practitioner may be very uncomfortable with having a foot in both camps. Most significant is the distinction between researching a system that may involve gathering data on others (many forms of AR and some forms of PAR) and collaboratively learning from the direct experience of participating in the inquiry. This is the subtle, yet significant, distinction raised by Kasl that "collaborative inquiry is research based in personal experience, not like an action research team that goes out to collect data from someone else" (E. Kasl, personal communication, 1996).

Another key distinction is the focus of PAR on problem solving (or, in the "Southern School," on liberation). The focus of a collaborative inquiry group is on understanding and constructing meaning around experience—a focus that may involve learning for purposes of personal development, enhancement of some aspect of one's practice, creating a new context for one's practice, or problem solving.

CI rests on a radical philosophy of knowledge that honors the "full range of human sensibilities as an instrument of research" (Heron, 1996, p. 7). This philosophy of knowledge has been most fully developed by Heron as a pyramid of knowing. At the base of the pyramid is experiential knowing (knowing through empathy and attunement with present experience). At the next level of the pyramid is presentational knowing (knowing through creative presentational forms such as graphics, drama, stories, and poetry). The third level is propositional knowing (expressed in the form of formal language). The pyramid culminates with practical knowing (the ability to change things through action).

Two points about this pyramid are of special interest to the theory of collaborative inquiry. First, the relationships of propositional knowing to practical knowing are reversed from the conventions of science, with practical knowing being viewed as the highest form of knowing built on the foundation of the other three. This reverses the traditional academic model that holds propositional knowledge as the highest, and most valued, form of knowing.

Second, an important validity check in collaborative inquiry is the congruence or correspondence among the four types of knowing. This contrasts with traditional notions of validity that center on the way propositional constructs are measured.

A third way in which collaborative inquiry differs from both traditional AR and many forms of PAR is the definition of the CI group being a group of peers in terms of answering the question. Here CI, as we understand it, and McTaggart's (1997a) point about authentic participation are aligned. However, often in action research and PAR the "researchers" in the formal sense are better educated, at least in terms of research training. Although the goal of the researchers in PAR may be to help the group become self-determining, the differences in their formal training inevitably influence the direction of the inquiry. To a great extent the PAR model seems to involve a transfer of skills and abilities.

In CI the preferred goal is a group of peers. Members may bring a diverse set of skills and experiences to the group, but these are not viewed as the basis for early differentiation, and perhaps deference, among members. If the initiator is someone who has experience in CI and whose principal role is to help establish the group, the initiator is the person with the problematic role—a person who has to quickly concede authority as soon as possible during the inquiry. The assumption cannot be that the initiator has any long-term role in directing the group.

Action Science

Action science (AS) is a form of inquiry that has been developed by Chris Argyris and Donald Schon (1974), along with some of Argyris' students (Argyris, Putnam, & Smith, 1985). Growing out of the action research tradition of Lewin and the pragmatism of Dewey, essentially action science is "inquiry into how human beings design and implement action in relation to one another" (Argyris et al., 1990, p. 4). It is a science of practice, including professional practitioners, such as managers, educators, or the like, and the practice of everyday living in families, social organizations, and communities. People practicing in AS participate in a structured and data centered process of public reflection. This process is directed toward understanding and acting on the causes that result in people consistently creating outcomes that they don't intend to create. The goal of the process is helping participants learn how to produce freely chosen alternative outcomes.

Action science, then, shares with action research a focus on examining the consequence of action and developing alternative ways of making action more effective. This is accomplished through a form of reflection. It also posits a theory of knowledge that holds that the most robust test of validity is whether or not the actions taken produce their intended consequences. Argyris (1996) calls this actionable knowledge—knowledge relevant to the world of practice and knowledge that people use to create their world.

Action science merges certain characteristics of traditional mainstream scientific inquiry with the concerns of the interpretive traditions of hermeneutics, phenomenology, and related forms of the human sciences (Argyris et al., 1985, ch. 1). With mainstream science it shares the values around generating "empirically disconfirmable propositions that are organized into a theory" (p. 4). Argyris and his colleagues see as central to AS the core elements of traditional scientific practice—the use of hard data, explicit inferences, empirically disconfirmable propositions and systematic theory. With the human sciences AS shares the notion that human beings create the meanings that they then use to guide their actions in everyday life. One cannot just observe the regularities among social events and arrive at an understanding of these meanings—and hence an understanding of the events themselves. Action science converts the meanings understood by social actors into hard data that are publicly accessible for purposes of rigorous testing.

This is accomplished through the use of specific methods developed over the years by Argyris and his close colleague, Donald Schon. People are trained in AS through the use of cases that descriptively reproduce, as accurately as possible, actual problematic interactions they have experienced. Using specific action science methods, the case is analyzed to reveal how their own behavior was being based on untested attributions and thus constructing the unproductive exchange.

As a form of action inquiry, AS subscribes to the same democratic values as participatory action research. Its goal is to convert communities of practice into communities of inquiry through the use of action science methodology. In this, AS is firmly rooted in the pragmatic tradition of Dewey who advocated the application of the scientific method in the pursuit of resolving practical problems.

From Action Science to Action Inquiry

Action science is a very rational and cognitive practice. Although it acknowledges and incorporates into its practice the critique made of traditional mainstream science found in the hermeneutic and human science literature, it is firmly rooted in the primary values of mainstream science. Its goal is to create a rigorous social science of "actionable knowledge" that adheres to these primary values. In that sense it is an extension of traditional social science. Propositional knowledge remains the highest form of knowing, although producing effective action is the most rigorous test of this knowledge.

An extension and elaboration of action science is the action inquiry (AI) approach of William Torbert (1981, 1987, 1991; Fisher & Torbert, 1995). Action inquiry incorporates the methods of action science into its practice, especially the analysis of cases and dialogue. However, it differs significantly in its orientation toward data and validity.

The focus of action inquiry is enhanced holistic awareness during action—"'consciousness' in the midst of action . . . is . . . both the ultimate aim and the primary research instrument in action inquiry" (Torbert, 1991, p. 221). For Torbert and his colleagues consciousness is marked by a widened attention embracing what he calls the four territories of experience; intuition, reason, one's own action, and the outside world.

At the center of action inquiry is "primary data" that are encountered "on-line in the midst of perception and action" (p. 221). Awareness of how one is experiencing the outside world, one's own behavior, reactions, and thought processes is primary. Data collected through instrumentation are afforded secondary attention and employed to challenge, support, and/or bring a fuller attention to primary data. Secondary data are always tested against the primary data of experience, in an extreme form of member checks, rather than the other way around.

Developing this awareness requires attention not only to events but also to one's feelings and thought processes in the process of acting. The heart of action inquiry is reflection in action—ongoing consciousness of how one is feeling and thinking and how one's feeling and thinking is facilitating or inhibiting his or her intention. This awareness is developed both through cognitive analysis of cases of personal interactions and through meditative practice.

Although action inquiry shares with action science the goal of creating communities of inquiry, it goes beyond the boundaries of AS. For

Torbert the practice of action inquiry is a way of life; the professional and personal are inseparable. This fusion of the professional and personal is distressing to those action-oriented researchers who still hold to the central values of traditional mainstream social science. In his forward to Torbert's *The Power of Balance* (1991), Donald Schon acknowledges this as he writes, "What I find most disconcerting. . . is Torbert's refusal to respect conventional boundaries between personal and professional life" (p. xiii). The methods of action inquiry are for Torbert "a kind of scientific inquiry that is conducted in everyday life" (p. 220).

The distinction between action science and action inquiry is expressed by Torbert, a former student of Argyris, and for years a close colleague of both Argyris and Schon, in his preface to his book. Recalling a conversation among the three, Torbert writes that he recognized that he viewed their work together differently than Argyris and Schon. "As empirically based as all of our work is, I viewed their work and my four previous books as pointing toward a fundamentally different frame or paradigm of social science from the natural social science paradigm. . . . They, on the other hand, both stressed the continuity between their work and the natural science paradigm of empirical disconfirmability" (p. viii). Action inquiry is a rigorously developed form of participative human inquiry.

The heightened competencies of reflection-in-action on intentional behavior involving cognitive and emotional capacities are facilitative of the practice of collaborative inquiry. Developing this awareness is helpful in both the action and collaborative reflection phases of the process. So, too, is the attention to stories and myths that surround one's experience and the attention to how we frame our comments and balance dialogue among advocacy, illustration, and inquiry. Collaborative inquiry is research into lived experience and Torbert's work provides skill sets and directions that are very applicable to the learning and development that takes place within it.

Action Learning

Unfortunately, the term "action learning" has been appropriated by trainers in the United States to refer to a wide range of learning activities including simulations, outdoor adventure experiences, and task force work. However valuable these activities may or may not be, it is important to distinguish them from the action learning tradition. The seminal work in action learning was done by Reg Revans (1982), an English physicist who was charged with the responsibility for management development for the British coal mines during a time of industrial crisis in the 1930s (O'Neil & Marsick, 1994). Revans evolved a model of learning that differentiated between programmed knowledge from the past (which he labeled P learning) and questioning insight (which he labeled Q learning). The former could be learned through reading books and listening to lectures; the latter could be developed only through wrestling with complex problems confronting people, taking action on these problems, and reflecting on the results. Revans formalized his approach in the form of action learning "sets"—small groups that work on solving real problems through repeated cycles of action and reflection.

Learning through the reinterpretation of the learner's own experience, without the knowledge imparted by an educator, was the focus of Revans' approach (Pedler, 1991). Each member of the set brings a problem that he or she is working toward resolving. Through the use of questions to foster insight, the other set members help one another learn from the previous actions. Alternatively, the set may work on a common problem, using their time together for reflection and dialogue.

Several schools of action learning have evolved over time (Yorks, O'Neil, & Marsick, 1999). The set model has been elaborated by others to include a learning coach. The role of this learning coach is to facilitate the reflective process by helping the set members stay focused on asking reflective questions as opposed to giving advice, although the use of a facilitator is seen as contingent on the needs of the set (McGill & Beaty, 1995). Others have extended Revans' original model to emphasize the interaction between P & Q learning (Mumford, 1997).

Independent of Revans, the Management Institute of Lund (MiL) in Sweden developed its own form of action learning called Action Reflection Learning (ARL)™ in which managers work in teams on projects in companies or businesses other than their own (Marsick & Cederholm, 1988). Equal emphasis is given to using the team as a vehicle for learning and for working on the project. As indicated by the name, more emphasis is placed on learning to learn through reflection than is found in many other variations of action learning. The ARL™ model was introduced into the United States by Leadership in International Management, Ltd.

Both forms of action learning develop insight into real world problems, foster critical thinking, and provide development of various forms of interpersonal competence. Traditional action learning has as its primary goal individual learning and development. Because of its organizational context ARL™ involves learning at the individual, group, and organizational levels.

Both models of action learning are distinct from collaborative inquiry, however. In the traditional set model, individuals work on their own question or problem, assisted through a process of factual, reflective, and interpretative questions raised by the other members of the group. Each member of the set gets to hold "air time" with their individual issue.

In the ARL™ model, a team works on a common question or project. This project is typically sponsored by an executive from the organization that has the problem. In the American ARL™ model the sponsor is from the same organization as the members of the team. In the Swedish model, team members are drawn from different organizations than the one sponsoring the project. In either case the team is working on a client problem, rather than its own. Although action learning teams experience many of the same group learning dynamics as a collaborative inquiry group the context is not the same. Since team members are nominated by their organizations for participation in the process, participation, while usually considered to be a good opportunity for learning and career advancement, is not self-initiated. This undoubtedly influences which opportunities for learning are pursued by the group.

Action learning is a powerful adult learning strategy with many similarities to CI. However, it is applicable in settings very different from CI and for different purposes. The essential differences are found in the context of AL, which often involves an organizational sponsored set of questions, or the individual question of each set member, and the frequent use of a learning coach.

Appreciative Inquiry

One of the newest approaches to organizational and social system intervention is appreciative inquiry. Its hopeful thesis is that "appreciation is a powerful reality-producing perspective and that when seen collectively through new eyes, our organizations can be vitally transformed in ways that eclipse anything the modernist world has yet known"

(Srivastva, Fry, & Cooperrider, 1990, p. 1). Appreciative inquiry is at once explicitly constructivist in nature, while tracing its roots to "the Lewinian premise that human action is critically dependent on the world as perceived rather than the world as it is" (p. 1).

Appreciative inquiry takes as one of its beginning points the assertion that the focus of action research, and by extension much organizational development practice, has been problem driven. This problem-solving focus has been limiting because it focuses on fixing what is rather than imagining the possibilities of what could be. The most powerful force in creating new organizational and social contexts is held to be the perspective that powerful actors bring to a situation—perspective produces behavior that enacts it own reality.

Writers in this emerging tradition view it as a form of participatory inquiry that honors intuition as well as analysis, holism as well as reductionism, and consciousness as the primary causal agent in everyday life experience (Harman, 1990; Sperry, 1981). Appreciative inquiry does not deny the accomplishments of traditional mainstream science, but argues that taken alone each is insufficient to produce a social system that fulfills human potential. Harman (1990) advances a model built on Popper's (Popper & Eccles, 1981) analogy of a bookshelf with three shelves; the physical science shelf with books that depict nature as deterministic and explanations that are reductionistic; the second shelf with life science books that include more holistic concepts like organism and system function; and a third shelf of human sciences with even more holistic concepts such as consciousness, culture, and life-world. The concepts contained in the books on each higher level shelf are not completely reducible to the level below. To this library Harman adds a fourth shelf of spiritual sciences that "deal with subjective reports of deep inner experience" as "achieved in meditative states" and choices guided "by some kind of deep intuition" (Harman, 1990, p. 48). Harman's fourth shelf of science has been approached by some forms of phenomenology and Gestalt psychology.

Appreciative inquiry shares with action inquiry a concern with the dynamics of leadership and power. Writers in this emerging form of action inquiry, emphasize the spiritual dimension of leadership and the artful aspects of seeing the possibilities in a situation that logical-empirical formulation of the setting would define as problematic (Mirvis, 1990). As a form of research, appreciative inquiry has been offered as a process of creative meaning-making through reflection on data and theory that are situationally determined (Cooperrider &

Srivastva, 1987). Harman (1990) asserts that *"a willingness to be trans-*
formed is an essential characteristic of the participatory scientist. . . .
scientists who would study in . . . 'spiritual science' have to be willing to
go through the deep changes that will make them competent observers"
(p. 48). In its intent and practice, appreciative inquiry is consistent with
Torbert's action inquiry and is *simpatico* with the practice of collaborative inquiry. In its present form, however, it has developed more as a
form of organizational intervention and leadership than as a broad-
based form of human inquiry.

AN INVITATION TO PRACTICE
COLLABORATIVE INQUIRY

As we have seen, there are arrays of action inquiry methodologies for
facilitating learning, initiating change, and conducting research. Distinctions among these methodologies are selected critical dimensions
summarized in Table 3.1. We have also included a column in the table
on traditional classroom training and seminar learning events to high-
light the distinction between action-oriented methods as learning interventions and classroom learning.

Among the action methodologies, collaborative inquiry holds its
place as a fully collaborative method for practicing inquiry into questions of shared importance among all the participants. It can be
employed to explore questions of inner human experience, personal
development, building community, and improving practice. Collaborative inquiry is one of the least hierarchical of the action strategies—
indeed it is nonhierarchical in its organization and it should be practiced
free from external coercion. Members of an inquiry can, however, share
an organizational context and be inquiring into how they can be more
effective in that context. An example is the group of secondary school
teachers in upstate New York (Bray, 1995) inquiring into the question,
"How can we improve our practice by becoming more of a community?"
Collaborative inquiry is also a methodology in which formal knowledge
is constructed that contributes to broader theory (Group for Collaborative Inquiry & thINQ, 1994). This is accomplished systematic examina-
tion of data and lived experience, using open dialogue and paying close
attention to potential threats to validity. The learning is shared with
larger publics. Making this happen is challenging. When we first started
practicing collaborative inquiry we had the aid of existing models but

TABLE 3.1 Summary of Distinctions Between Action Inquiry Methodologies and Classroom Learning

	Collaborative Inquiry	Appreciative Inquiry	Participatory Action Research	Action Science	Action Inquiry	Training Approaches to Learning
Purpose	Knowledge production/meaning. Research using experience and development of community (or teams).	Strategy productions using positive experiences and imaginative thinking of its members.	Change at individual and societal levels.	Change at individual and organizational levels. Learning in terms of avoiding the production of outcomes that participants seek to avoid.	Change at individual and organizational levels through in-the-moment awareness of how actions and emotions are impacting effectiveness.	Skill building. Information dissemination.
Group Size	Usually 5 to 12 people, may be clustered into a federation of several CI groups.	Varies from small- to large-group interventions.	Varies from small- to large-group interventions.	Varies from individual-to-group and organizational interventions.	Varies from individual-to-group and organizational interventions.	Varies. Can be very large. Increasing focus on distance learning.

(continued)

TABLE 3.1 (Continued)

	Collaborative Inquiry	Appreciative Inquiry	Participatory Action Research	Action Science	Action Inquiry	Training Approaches to Learning
Facilitator Role	Likely to initiate the group. Role shifts into a co-inquirer, co-learner role in which leadership is shared.	Group process expert, experienced in use of the appreciative inquiry model.	Organizer/ researcher knowledgeable in a wide range of research methods and group process methodology. Often knowledgeable in the problem area being researched. In Southern school often knowledgeable in theories of transformative social change and learning theories.	Observer/ researcher, knowledgeable in inquiry methods that bring forward assumptions and test them against empirical data. Confronts participant's assumptions and maps consequences of assumptions and actions.	Observer/ researcher. Encourages the use of effective speech acts and cognitive and emotional awareness, often through meditation exercises.	Content expert, likely to have group process skills.

few specifics on how to operationalize them. We had to create our methods as we went along. The chapters that follow are intended as a guide for those who wish to practice this type of inquiry. It is not dogma. Indeed, one of the values of collaborative inquiry is the avoidance of dogmatic methods, keeping the methods of inquiry open. However, one must be willing to engage others in dialogue about one's approach and methods to justify the meaning that emerges as valid. The meaning of validity is itself a serious topic for inquiry. Our hope is that this book will assist others in engaging in this type of inquiry as part of their academic programs, in their professional practice, and in other venues of experience. We also hope that they, too, share their experience and methods in the public arena.

4

Forming a Collaborative Inquiry Group

Everyone interested in participating in collaborative inquiry initially ponders the question, "How does one go about conducting a collaborative inquiry?" We now turn our attention to the primary purpose of this book—providing a map for those who wish to initiate and participate in collaborative inquiry as a method for conducting both human inquiry and adult learning. In a sense, this is a paradoxical task. There are no hard-and-fast guidelines for conducting a collaborative inquiry, at least not in the traditional sense of a research orthodoxy. Such an orthodoxy would be contrary to the spirit of openness and learning that is the basis of CI. The only constraints governing CI are the values of collaboration and participation described in Chapter 1 and the requirement that claims to new knowledge should be open to further inquiry in the public arena. Knowledge claims must be supported by full disclosure of methods and validity criteria.

What is the purpose of the map if not to provide a set of prescriptive methodological guidelines? Its purpose is to provide a detailed, experientially based discussion of the paths available and choices that confront those who chose to embark on this kind of inquiry. There is a growing case literature describing variations of participatory human inquiry (Reason, 1988b, 1994b), and the theoretical framing of cooperative inquiry is becoming more complete (Heron, 1996). However, there is still a gap between the theoretical framing of cooperative inquiry and the case literature in terms of providing concrete guidance as to specific steps that can be taken in carrying out this kind of inquiry. Providing this guidance is the primary purpose of this book. We use the term *guidance* in its most liberal interpretation—providing direction without authoritarian stricture. Our expectation is that this form of inquiry stands to be significantly enriched as others add their voices of experience to its practice. No form of inquiry can flourish in the absence of healthy dialogue about methods.

We begin our discussion with the first phase of a collaborative inquiry: forming a collaborative inquiry group. This phase is crucial to the future effectiveness of the inquiry, since passion and excitement drive the collaborative inquiry process. Passion and excitement are initially jarring words to characterize a research effort. Words such as *dispassion* and *distancing* characterize the manuals of conventional research. This idea of dispassion is, of course, mythology. Most groundbreaking research, regardless of paradigm, is marked by passion on the part of the principal researchers, and usually many of their assistants as well. The prescriptive vision of the dispassionate researcher is a methodological consideration, not a motivational one. The prescription for emotional distancing of the researcher from his or her subjects is based on concerns about researchers infusing their subjects with enthusiasm or otherwise jeopardizing the validity of their studies. Furthermore, it rests on the assumption that social scientists can somehow transcend their own social setting and position within their society and achieve a totally objective stance. Ultimately, this concern with objectivity has to do with preventing the self-delusion of the researchers and others who rely on their conclusions.

As discussed in Chapter 1, we believe the idea that social researchers are truly objective is itself a form of delusion, and that the methodological stances it leads to cuts off researchers from valuable understanding of human experience. We do share with our more traditional colleagues concern for misunderstanding our experience. Validity tests are part of the CI process. However, in initiating the inquiry, the motivational concerns of all involved are important.

In collaborative inquiry, the distinction between researcher and subject is eliminated. The goal in getting started is establishing a group of co-researchers/co-subjects who share a burning desire for new knowledge and a willingness to work with others to pursue new avenues of meaning. Successfully accomplished, this group consensus can provide the impetus for creating a unique learning experience.

INITIATING A
COLLABORATIVE INQUIRY GROUP

The decision to initiate a collaborative inquiry group is often part of a complex inner struggle. Unlike conventional research, where questions are largely theory driven, or traditional action research, where problems are held by a client, the inspiration for conducting a collaborative inquiry often comes from some disquiet rooted in one's own experience. This disquiet may stem from some dilemma of professional practice or a sense of curiosity about how to improve or initiate change in an aspect of one's life. Or it may be inwardly centered on a not fully formulated need for exploration into one's private sense of being. The disquiet can be around an intellectual question or rooted in the problems of life.

Rowan (1981) suggests that the decision to initiate this kind of inquiry is likely to begin when individuals experience an imbalance or disequilibrium in their state of being. He describes this imbalance as moving from resting in one's experience to a sense of dissatisfaction with one's practice (Rowan, cited in Reason, 1988c, p. 7). In phenomenological terms, a part of one's life-world becomes negated, but instead of retreating into feelings of defensiveness and displacement, curiosity is aroused.

Translation of this curiosity into collaborative inquiry is itself not an easy process. The individual's enthusiasm for an inquiry must be confronted by issues raised by working with others in a highly collaborative way. One has to seriously consider whether one wishes to engage in a cooperative quest, as opposed to a more individualistic approach with its promise of maintaining control over the process of learning from experience and where that might lead.

Grounding in one's sense of being is an important concept. Successfully establishing a collaborative inquiry group is highly dependent on the initiator who has the nagging idea or feeling of disquiet about a situation. An initiator goes through a transition from thinking about the issue to acting on it through a process of inquiry. Since collaborative inquiry is a process of learning from experience, the initiator needs to ground the original question in his or her experience. Determining whether one is prepared to experientially explore the question is a process of aligning one's thoughts with one's feelings, one's practice with one's theory and beliefs. To what extent is one willing to contrast his or her experience with that of others? And to what extent is one willing to engage in personal exposure around the question? The prospect of learning is often exciting; the commitment to forming a group may be, for some, daunting. The first test is the process of initiating and informing.

INITIATING THE INQUIRY THROUGH CONFERRING WITH OTHERS

Forming a collaborative inquiry group requires a substantial commitment of time and energy. The process itself is contextually situated. In some cases, the initiator may be soliciting interest in a setting where initially there appears to be little interest. His or her solicitation may stimulate interest in the same question from some potential participants. In other settings, the initiator may tap into an existing stream of interest and galvanize others to pursue their interests collectively rather than individually. In either case, the initiator's action of inviting others to participate in an inquiry represents a dual test—the extent to which the general topic of concern resonates with the experience of others and the appeal of engaging in this form of inquiry.

In our work, initiators have used various approaches to invite participation and to establish a group: announcements circulated among a specific population of potential participants, phone calls or face-to-face conversations with persons who fit a profile of a possible participant, and even informal interviews. In inviting participants, the initiator walks a line between conveying a sense of enthusiasm for the inquiry and maintaining a low-key, unforced, informing approach. In collaborative inquiry, the group members are to a certain extent self-organizing, arranging to meet based on their perceived mutual needs. As the initiator creates opportunities to explore options for participation, relationships develop among prospective participants even before the inquiry actually begins.

The invitation to form an inquiry group on the application of technology in education was made to the members of a state task force of 50 technology leaders at the end of a year-long project (Gerdau, 1995). (Summaries of the inquiries referred to in this chapter are in Box 1.1, Chapter 1.) Joyce distributed a memorandum detailing the purpose of the collaborative inquiry and its proposed topic, inviting members to extend their collaboration to a specific topic. In contrast, Linda initiated a collaborative inquiry of peer counselors through conversational meetings with members of the community women's group (Smith, 1995). Informational materials were distributed in a context of personal intimacy. The members of the intuition in teaching group were approached individually (Zelman, 1995). The group's initiator engaged a number of faculty members in conversation, describing what she hoped to do. Whether the invitation to participate is issued in writing or verbally, the initiator must devise an approach that is congruent with the interests of the participants and is appropriate to the culture.

Co-Initiation

It is possible to engage in a two-step process, with the initiator first exploring the possibilities of an inquiry with one or two colleagues who share his or her concerns. This may actually begin as part of the transition from feeling a sense of disquiet or interest in a question to moving toward action. While turning to a trusted friend or colleague for advice and "brainstorming" the possibilities, they agree to become co-initiators. This approach was taken in initiating the group of university faculty inquiring into how they might get students to take more responsibility for their learning in a way that makes the university more of a learning organization (Yorks, 1995). Lyle, the initiator, began having discussions with a colleague who shared his interest in learning organizations and the paradox that the university seemed impervious to innovation in the way it structured its curriculum. Further discussion revealed a shared concern about how passive many of the students were and a recognition of a possible connection between the observations about the university and about the students. These discussions led to an agreement to co-initiate an inquiry. They began to formulate the inquiry question, "How can we help students take more responsibility for their learning in a way that makes the university more of a learning organization?"

Out of their discussions emerged the explicit assumption that many of the actions that might be taken would require interaction with the organizational system. The two expanded their dialogue to involve a third member who held a position of influence within the organization. It was important that he was able to accept collegial equality (as opposed to hierarchical authority) around the question. He joined the two as a third co-initiator. Together the three co-initiators were able to anticipate the institutional contextual factors that might have an impact on the project. All three initiators participated in identifying teaching and administrative faculty who they believed might share their interest.

Obtaining Institutional Consent

While some collaborative inquiries require no institutional support, many require at least tacit support. The reasons may be related either to the composition of the group or to the expectation of participants that the actions they take during the inquiry will involve altering institutional practices.

Gaining support from institutional decision-makers takes time and knowledge of how innovative projects are successfully initiated within the organization in question. This requires an understanding of the institutional culture. Institutional support is gained through persistence and the development of a trustworthy relationship. It is necessary to move the proposal from what may be considered by key organizational stakeholders as an interesting idea to an initiative that is of value to the institution. There is an art to this positioning of CI, which involves emphasis on the developmental potential both for participants in the inquiry and for an organization. This needs to be done without compromising the inquiry process by promising specific outcomes.

For example, the group of secondary school teachers exploring how they might build a better sense of community needed both time and a place to meet (Bray, 1995). John extended an invitation to the school's faculty. Exactly one-half responded, resulting in a relatively large inquiry group of eight participants. Obtaining a time and place for this group to meet on regular basis was a challenge.

Prior to initiating this inquiry, John knew he would need the support of the district superintendent on four issues. First, he needed the superintendent's consent to allow teachers to commit to the inquiry process. This was required because of the initiators' second need: the use of inquiry as a substitute for professional in-service education time. John believed that asking teachers to donate large blocks of after-school time was both unreasonable (especially given the large amounts of time already given to preparation and extracurricular activities) and unprofessional. Thus, released time was needed, and this would necessitate the hiring of substitute teachers to cover the classes of those attending inquiry meetings. Third, because the school did not have a conference room, the inquiry group needed an off-site meeting location. This in turn necessitated arrangements for meals. School policy states that when teachers attend off-site conferences during school hours, they have their meals paid for by the school. Finally, John wanted copies of *Human*

Inquiry in Action (Reason, 1998b) to provide a common theoretical grounding for those participating in the inquiry.

John approached the district superintendent to explain the inquiry as a very active and innovative way of fostering staff development. He suggested it would be more productive than the traditional practice of bringing in outside speakers to lecture to the teachers on topics that the teachers had little or no voice in selecting, in a setting where they had even less opportunity to participate in formulating the agenda. The superintendent was wholly in favor of the idea, saying that involving teachers in the improvement of their profession was an innovative practice that he wholeheartedly supported. He did not place limits on the size of the group and approved sufficient funding for six meetings: 2 full days and 4 half-days to be spaced throughout the academic year.

Having obtained the support of the superintendent, John set out to test the waters prior to issuing his invitation to the faculty. He discussed the idea of collaborative inquiry with three faculty members, describing some of the inquiries reported in the Reason book and emphasizing that this kind of a project would be a significant departure from past in-service education practices at the school. The group would collaboratively formulate its inquiry question and then engage in repeated cycles of action and reflection on it. Its one purpose would be the improvement of their practice as teaching professionals. When he asked them directly, "Is this a form of in-service education you are interested in pursuing?" all three said yes. Having now obtained preliminary approval from the superintendent and at least the nucleus of a group, he prepared to move forward with a formal invitation at the beginning of the coming school year.

The invitation was made through a presentation John made at the general faculty meeting during the call for many committees to be established. He presented a synopsis of the proposed collaborative inquiry project, including an explanation of the CI process; cited the reasons he believed the research was warranted; and extended an invitation to everyone to participate.

The collaborative inquiry with community women required establishing a liaison between the peer counseling program and the public health agency sponsoring it (Smith, 1995). The support of the program coordinator was necessary to enable the inquiry meetings to "piggyback" onto regular monthly meetings. The peer counseling program was founded as a project of La Leche League International as an effort to expand the League's peer learning structure, which supports middle- and upper-income mothers in breastfeeding but involves few low-income mothers. The project works with the Supplemental Feeding Program for Women, Infants, and Children, a popular food and health program of the public health agency. At the time the inquiry was initiated, a cultural anthropologist who was a colleague of Linda's described it as appearing to be not a group "but a series of dyad relationships between individuals and the coordinator." The coordinator, however, was interested in helping the women in the program learn and grow and also was interested in the recognition the inquiry project might bring for the program's work. She agreed to help and expressed support for the inquiry.

In obtaining approval for initiating inquiries within an organizational context, it is important that the inquiry remain under control of the participants. There is a danger that institutional sponsors will be expecting a specific institutional gain in terms of the group's pursuing some course of action that management has predetermined it prefers. An important aspect of negotiating institutional support is that everyone understands that CI is an open process of research. Practices adopted to ensure the validity of the knowledge that emerges will enforce this principle. The importance of this requirement alone virtually guarantees that legitimate collaborative inquiry will not emerge as a fad in institutional settings, since administrators cannot assume that some preexisting conclusion on their part will emerge from the group. As one group of nervous senior managers realized before putting off such an effort, "People might start to question how things are done around here!" The initiator should keep in mind that the mark of a valid collaborative inquiry is that it has produced change in the participants—change is the marker of learning. Often this change results in new approaches to practice that affects organizational settings.

Establishing an inquiry project within a larger organizational context requires practitioners to consider a variety of factors. Each collaborative inquiry faces its own challenges and complexities, but when problems are confronted and not ignored or buried, the group creates a solid platform for forging ahead with its learning-oriented work. In planning inquiries that take place in professional, work, or other institutional settings, it is imperative that the initiator or initiators give careful thought to organizational issues. Indeed, once the group has formed and its question has been formulated, the participants should brainstorm the organizational factors likely to affect the inquiry process and progress.

Obtaining Consent From Participants

By its very nature, collaborative inquiry implies participant consent. The extended nature of the invitation and informing process, leading to the roles of co-participants and co-researcher shared by all participants, highlights the relationship and trust building that are hallmarks of the inquiry process. Nevertheless, human subject ethics committees will appropriately require that inquiries conducted in university and many other institutional settings have informed consent forms available to be signed. In contrast to more traditional research projects in which consent forms are signed as a preliminary task, collaborative inquiry initiators work through the permission process in more of a web-like manner. The extended process of informing participants about CI makes the signing of consent forms a very natural part of the agreement process when arriving at the point of deciding to join the inquiry.

In the six groups that formed the federated project led by members of thINQ, we developed a one-page consent form and had it signed at the point when each group agreed on the question and criteria for the inquiries. Looking back on the inquiry projects, the act of signing the forms was to the participants a procedural nicety, overshadowed by each co-inquirer's hope for learning about highly compelling issues.

Establishing the Physical Context of the Inquiry

Because of the open-ended quality of collaborative inquiry and its emphasis on partnership versus the researcher-subject relationship, the setting of the inquiry assumes critical importance. The considerations include not just assessing the physical setting or the environment where the prospective inquiry will take place, but also discovering and responding to the "genius loci," the spirit of the place—its history, values, and leadership. For example, initially the university group on organizational learning met in offices and conference rooms on campus, seated around conference tables. Later, the group met in the home of one of the members. The tone of the meetings changed, and the discussions became less institutionalized. Participants noted that leaving campus provided a mental break—the group no longer felt as much like a faculty committee or taskforce. They felt more energy.

Settings have ranged from training centers to conference rooms, university classrooms, church fellowship halls, and homes. For example, Joyce, initiator of the group on technology in the classroom, arranged for an "adult, rather than a child-centered ambiance" (Gerdau, 1995). As discussed above, the group of secondary teachers met off-site. The fact that the superintendent rented a meeting room at a nearby university added to the importance of the group and validated the project as professional development. The Intuition Group met in an off-the-beaten-track setting at the college, adding to the intimacy of the group (Zelman, 1995). For each setting the initiators considered the location and travel time; the comfort level of the atmosphere; the options for shifting furniture should the need arise; and access to food and restrooms. They also looked for a setting where there would be a minimum of disruption, to guarantee that the participants could be attentive to the group and not easily distracted. An appropriate context establishes a relatively secure, relaxed environment. The setting should provide a "psychological space" that enables the group to separate itself from outside cares and concerns.

Ensuring Diversity

One important consideration in issuing the invitation is recruiting for breadth. The inclusion of differing views is not just an asset to the collaborative process but a necessity. In our work as a collaborative inquiry group, we valued diversity by acknowledging divergent communication and learning styles, knowing that these differences contributed to the richness of our inquiry. In other inquiries, we recruited participants from different backgrounds, with a variety of skills and experiences. In the inquiry of community women, cultural diversity was an integral part of the experience.

In the early phases of a collaborative inquiry, the initiator can unlock the diversity of the group by encouraging the use of personal experience and viewpoints. This enlightens and informs each participant about the commonalities and divergence within the group. Many preconceptions and misconceptions are dispelled in this manner, and this process helps to establish a norm of valuing diversity and the divergence of perspective it brings to the inquiry.

The life history model used by the teachers group is a good example of unlocking diversity (Bray, 1995). The teachers engaged in rounds of storytelling about their professional history and the reasons each had chosen to work in this particular school. In a similar but more condensed manner, the inquiry group of technology experts drew from different work settings such as school, government, and community college to explore past experiences relevant to the potential inquiry question (Gerdau, 1995). In the community women's group, the women shared a meal of their favorite foods from their different cultures to link individual past experience and the group's diversity to collaborative inquiry.

While there is a limit to the effective size of collaborative inquiry group, the number is not fixed. Somewhere between five and twelve appears to be the number that allows for diversity, while still allowing the group to function democratically and with reasonable efficiency. Particularly with adult learners, whose lives and problems are complex, each member greatly increases the difficulty of scheduling times and places convenient to all. On the positive side, large-scale interest and participation implies a truly compelling question.

An interesting alternative for an initiator confronted with a larger number of interested participants is to consider utilizing a federated model (P. Reason, personal communication, 1992). Several collaborative inquiry groups can be created with each group functioning independently of the others, but with a mechanism in place for communicating and sharing the learning among them. This obviously places more demands on the initiator and in most instances would require a group of co-initiators. More will be said about the potential for this kind of model in the final chapter.

ORIENTING THE GROUP

A newcomer to collaborative inquiry is likely to have many questions about the process. Indeed, those who have participated in previous groups are likely to have questions about the intentions of the initiator and how he or she initially envisions the group. An informational meeting in which participants can ask questions without having to declare their intent to participate at that time is recommended. During this informational session, it is important to explore with others the interests of prospective members and the expectations they hold for the group. It is a time for all to share assumptions about why they wish to participate and what they hope to gain from the experience. Potential participants will not only want to hear more about the research question and how it sparked initiation; they will want to ask questions about the collaborative inquiry process, learn more about the interests of prospective members, and gauge the potential synergy of the group. Doubts and concerns can surface and be addressed.

It is important for the initiator to remember that the potential participants are going through the same kind of transition process, from awareness to taking action through inquiry, that he or she went through. From the time the participants received the initial invitation to the time of the informational meeting, the question and the possibility of engaging in an inquiry was gestating in their minds. The fact that they initially responded positively to the invitation and took time to show up at the first meeting indicates that the question and the idea of collaborative inquiry resonated with them in some way. It is important that the meeting be structured in such a way that the potential participants have a chance to move toward making an informed decision about further participation.

During the information sessions we have held we have wanted to encourage potential participants in their decision about whether or not to join the collaboration. We have had a few very broad goals for our information meetings, including (a) emphasizing the expanded opportunities for participation and an authentic group experience, (b) introducing a tentative research question and devoting time for openly exploring it, (c) providing a glimpse into the potential synergy of the process, and (d) establishing ground rules for collaboration consistent with the central tenet of working *with* people.

Using an agenda that allows people to share what has brought them to the meeting—what they understand the question to be and why it's important to them, along with some background information—is appropriate. The initiator can then segue into a brief description of his or her own journey to this point—why he or she decided to initiate the group—and introduce the concept of collaborative inquiry. This presentation should allow for an open exchange between the initiator and the others. Next, the meeting needs to be thrown open for discourse among the potential participants. If the number of people is relatively large, the initiator may opt to facilitate this by first encouraging small-group discussion.

During the information session, prospective participants may or may not be aware of the differences between more traditional group processes and collaborative inquiry. Most working Americans are acculturated to meetings that emphasize sharply focused, problem-solving interactions. Such traditional meetings center on detailed structure, prescribed objectives, step-by-step agendas, and chairperson control. While this approach is appropriate and effective for many of the meetings held in organizations on a routine basis, it often proves inadequate for solving some of the more abstract, but profound, issues confronting contemporary organizations. In collaborative inquiry, during the first informational meeting, decisions may not be made, objectives may not be presented, and discussion may meander through rounds of informal conversation about relevant, and even irrelevant, topics. As will be related in a later chapter, this same meandering process often marks some of the most relevant learning during an inquiry.

For those fond of crisp, efficient orientations, this process may prove confusing and frustrating. It is important for practitioners to understand that the process requires departing from some traditional norms of group formation. The group should be aware of this shift into a freewheeling, exploratory, generative model of interpersonal interactions. Often experienced as random, messy, and divergent, the ambiguity experienced is intrinsic to an inquiry conducted by equals—participating, not leading; interacting, not observing.

It may be necessary to schedule two or three meetings before people are asked to commit, especially if the inquiry is to take place over an extended period of time. Some participants may need to attend a couple of sessions to make up their minds as they go through the transition process. In these instances, the second or third meeting can be devoted to further exploration of the collaborative inquiry process and clarifying potential participants' interest in the question. Depending on the tone of the group, the initiator may lead the group in surfacing the expectations they have of the group. (In this situation, the additional informational meetings may blend into the contracting phase. This is an organic, not mechanistic, process.) At the end of the informational session or sessions, however, it is time for prospective participants to make a commitment to the group. What constitutes commitment may vary from group to group, but the assumptions must be shared and adopted by all members. In other words, they must commit to one another and begin developing the inquiry project.

DEVELOPING THE INQUIRY PROJECT

Once participants have committed to the inquiry, the real work of the group begins. A number of important tasks lie immediately ahead. As a group, they must agree on the initial wording of the question, clarify their understanding of it, and design their vision of how they are going to go about answering it. It is during this stage that the initiator (or co-initiators) must begin another transition, going from initiator(s) and implied leadership to co-inquirer(s). The process of establishing the conditions for group learning—the topic of Chapter 5—begins in earnest at this time. Hence, the line between forming the group and establishing the conditions for group learning is not fixed but fluid and overlapping. Whether the group first refines the criteria that they agree will define their collaborative inquiry group and how it will operate or first frames their question is somewhat dependent on the setting. Generally, we have found that framing the question comes first, since the question may influence the criteria that are adopted.

Framing the Question

Virtually all organized research begins with a question. This is a basic postulate of research practice, attesting to the importance of asking the right question before becoming consumed with issues of methodology and design.

Although the participants were initially approached with an idea for the inquiry framed as a question, it is important to now give the question some serious collective thought. Often the question will become altered to more accurately capture the disjuncture or part of the life-world that is really stimulating the group. This process of sculpting the question starts the learning process. In the university learning organization group, there was much discussion around the differences between participating in a sequence of classroom experiences versus being a member of a campus community. A member of the group suggested that maybe the group needed a better definition of what was meant by "more responsibility." For an action step, the group agreed that before the next meeting each member would develop a definition of what he or she thought was meant by "taking responsibility for one's own learning."

In the intuition group, the original wording of the question underwent modification; the original emphasis on how intuition was used in teaching and learning changed to emphasize, instead, how the participants might nurture, promote, or foster intuition (Zelman, 1995). This more open-ended wording permitted the group to examine intuition in themselves, without precluding exploring its use in the classroom. One member was uncomfortable with the word "promote" in the question; "nurture" and "foster" seemed better choices. Reflecting the nature of the topic itself, the group resisted having a fixed, rigidly stated question. As the group developed, the wording was reiterated informally, sometimes with reference to the classroom, but most often referring to the broader issue of nurturing. There is typically a dynamic relationship between the question and the learning of the group, leading to a revision of the original question during the inquiry itself.

In our own inquiry into how learning is experienced in collaborative inquiry, our process of framing our question involved a lot of linguistic questioning and challenging assumptions. Considerable discussion was devoted to the use of "learning" versus "individual and group learning" and the sequencing of learning versus inquiry in terms of the relative emphasis being placed on the question. Going individually around the group, we each agreed to the question, "How are personal and group learning produced by the collaborative inquiry process?" Shortly thereafter, we replaced the word "personal" with "individual." As was related in Chapter 2, this question was again significantly reworded during our analysis phase.

Moving from individual learning interests to a group question. Progressing from the variety of individual learning interests that sparked a positive response to the invitation and information session, to formulating an inquiry question, constitutes a major step forward. The initiator must adopt a highly facilitative role in order to translate individual interests into a group question. Participants are likely to ask the initiator for guidance in accomplishing this. We have developed a number of strategies for doing so.

In our initial inquiry, we used brainstorming, first asking each member to bring a list of possible inquiry questions to the meeting as the basis for beginning the process. In the community women's inquiry, Linda asked for a round of stories about memorable experiences associated with peer counseling programs. As each person shared her story, critical words voicing the major ideas—problems, gaps, barriers, and peer counseling—were listed on newsprint. In this way, this group of culturally diverse women wrote the question, "What are the ways we can lower barriers to peer counseling?"

In the teacher's group, John facilitated a general discussion around the question as initially stated. Two of the teachers expressed their uneasiness with theoretical discourse, one of them saying that she had "blocked the use of theory out of my head when I left college." The other noted that theory as written text excludes vital pieces of the teaching experience—the flavor of the lived experience is lost as it is converted into writing. In the ensuing discussion, the group agreed that they wanted to improve their practice as teachers through direct investigation of techniques and strategies. This led to revision of the question to "How can we improve our practice by examining our practices?"

Joyce, the initiator of the technology integration group, asked each member to consider the broad parameters of the group's area of inquiry and come to the next meeting with an inquiry question or questions to be shared with the group. At the meeting, these questions were posted and discussed, prompting a freewheeling conversation ranging over a variety of issues that were affecting the preparation of educators for their new roles as technology managers and users. Following this lengthy discussion, Joyce reviewed the questions listed on the board and suggested that the group inquiry question "should give a holistic sense of what everyone's interests are." A member suggested that some of the questions could be "melded" into one another. This led to a process of wordsmithing that resulted in the framing of a question that the group felt represented progress, but still left the question somewhat elusive. Following a reflective silence, one member turned to Joyce and said, "You really need to decide how to word this," and the group agreed. Joyce said she would draft a tentative question that respected the spirit of the discussion. She would send it to all members before the next meeting so they could reflect on it and be prepared to challenge it. This led to further discussion at the next meeting resulting in agreement on the question.

Phrasing of the question. Framing a collaborative inquiry question requires careful attention to the limiting nature of certain words: "who," "when," and "where" suggest answers not requiring collaborative inquiry. It is important to avoid questions that have quantifiable or referenced answers. Collaborative inquiry is most effective addressing questions that are qualitative, experientially, and/or culturally based. They are most often phrased as "How can . . . ," "How do . . . ," and "What does . . . " type questions.

As presented in Chapter 1, an important consideration in phrasing the question is the extent to which it captures important or compelling concerns for all the participants and reflects their ability to take action on the question. In the spirit of inquiry, the question should remain open for revision, but revision based on rigorous reflection and experience, not frivolous changing interest. The question provides the parameters for designing the project.

Designing the Inquiry

Members of the group have to devise a plan for collaboratively answering their question. Approaches to project design will vary and are limited only by the group's creativity. The community women, for instance, discovered that their way of defining their inquiry question suggested the project design. The women used storytelling as a way of formulating their inquiry question; storytelling became a natural part of the inquiry project and their future interactions were enlivened by this mode of communication. The intuition group worked in a very fluid way, as one participant described it "not bound by regulation . . . by somebody setting down a set of rules" (Zelman, 1995, p. 216). They did, however, always come back to the inquiry question no matter how tangential they became (Zelman, 1995, pp. 216-217).

Any inquiry plan implies envisioning what the group's tasks should be and how they can best be accomplished by incorporating action and reflection within the time frames anticipated. The important elements of any plan include possible methods for answering the question, including kinds of actions and ways of capturing the experience in data/text form, expressive form, or both. Scheduling of meetings and the timing of the cycles of action and reflection are other important considerations. So, too, is how the meetings will be structured and the roles people will play, such as recording, agenda setting, facilitating, and time keeping.

There is an emergent, evolving aspect to the design phase. Members will project individual ideas while the collective thinking modifies what was earlier envisioned. During the design phase, group members raise many issues, advocate many approaches, and ask many questions.

As previously mentioned, in some cases the question gets reframed over time. This reframing may initiate a return to design options. Although cumbersome, such a return can produce a number of possibilities not necessarily evident at the outset of the inquiry.

BEGINNING THE TRANSITION FROM INITIATOR
TO CO-INQUIRER TO COLLECTIVE LEADERSHIP

Leadership is a significant issue for all groups. Yet collaborative inquiries are true leaderless groups. This paradox will be explored in more depth in Chapter 5. In this chapter (Chapter 4), we call attention to the fact that through the Forming phase, the initiator is playing an explicit leadership role. He or she has taken the initiative in convening the group. The group will be expecting the initiator to take the lead in organizing the informational meeting and to provide direction during contracting and project design activities. Yet, at the same time the initiator must take steps to ensure this is a truly collaborative effort.

This is not as easy as it sounds. As the group defines its criteria and shapes its question the initiator must be an active participant, but not carry a disproportionate weight in the decision-making process. There may be an expectation on the part of some, or even all, of the participants that the initiator will have the last word. They may repeatedly look to the initiator for affirmation that they are on the right track, and they may express anger toward the initiator when they first encounter the messiness of collaborative inquiry, expecting the initiator to lead them back on track. For his or her part, the initiator must not get possessive of the process if it goes in an unanticipated direction.

During this early stage of the project, the initiator should expect to play an organizing role, suggesting ways in which the group might get started, but then encouraging suggestions from others. During discussions of content, such as the adaptation of criteria or the wording of the question, the initiator must express him- or herself as a member of the group. If the initiator has a problem with some idea or wording, he or she must express it and explore it with the others as a member of the group. To withhold one's self is to disempower one's self and compromise the productivity of the group. On the other hand, every other member of the group must be afforded the same privilege.

As part of the planning stage, roles should be discussed. We rotated the role of facilitator, having that person prepare the draft agenda and take responsibility for timing and the overall organization of the meeting, with everyone taking responsibility for facilitating dialogue and discussion. In our other groups, we asked a member to also note periodic observations on the meeting's process and provide some descriptive feedback toward the end of the meeting for discussion. Through these kinds of mechanisms, a norm of distributive or collective leadership can be established.

There is one additional wrinkle that can influence this transition from initiator to co-inquirer. It involves the relationship of the initiator to the group in the most fundamental way. Ideally, the initiator is in a true peer relationship with the potential participants in the inquiry, relative to the question. He or she can fully participate in the experience. This is what Heron (1996) refers to as "full form cooperative inquiry." There are also instances of what he describes as partial form cooperative inquiry.

Partial form collaborative inquiry (Heron, 1996) occurs when all participants, including the initiator, are fully involved as co-researchers in the design of the inquiry and research reflections, but the initiator may be only partially involved as a co-subject. This form of inquiry occurs when one of the initiators is not a member of the community of practitioners from which the participants have been drawn. He or she may have been engaged as a consultant to help implement collaborative inquiry or otherwise have taken the initiative in getting members of a community of practice interested in CI as a learning strategy.

Heron (1996, pp. 23-24) suggests two ways of addressing this situation. One is for the initiator to become an "analogous co-subject" by carrying out parallel action in his or her own setting. This provides the basis for his or her participation in the group reflections. As an alternative to or in combination with this first approach, the initiator can visit the action sites of the other participants, making observations or engaging people in relevant opportunistic dialogue and conversational interviews. These data, however, are secondary to the experience of the actual co-subjects. This second option moves the initiator more toward the role of field researcher and must be carefully distinguished from the true co-subjects. These data may prove valuable, however, as a source of triangulation for the reflective dialogue in the group, stimulating different perspectives. On occasion, the data gathered in this way may provide for constructive devil's advocacy.

A third option is for the initiator to work with the group to get them started and then withdraw, perhaps periodically returning to answer questions about CI (as opposed to participating in the inquiry question). The group becomes a full form collaborative inquiry as the initiator withdraws.

In effect, Elizabeth Kasl played a partial role in our inquiry into how learning is experienced in collaborative inquiry. She issued the invitation and got us started. As time went by, she spent less time in our meetings, drawing on her ongoing experience in The Group for Collaborative Inquiry to raise questions about our process. During our analysis phase, she again attended several sessions, often playing a devil's advocate role.

Some of our most difficult feelings as initiators have centered on this issue of transitioning from initiator to co-inquirer. Effectively walking this line is one of the important components of forging a group learning culture, the focus of Chapter 5.

REFLECTING ON THE PROCESS

Chapter 5 discusses the question of establishing the conditions for group learning and a group culture that supports it. As noted previously, this process starts as group begins framing its question and developing a design for the inquiry. One of the most important behaviors that a group can adopt to help establish a climate for group learning is periodic reflection on its process. At the conclusion of important tasks, such as framing the question or making decisions about design, it is helpful if the group pauses for reflection. A few moments can be taken for each member to individually and quietly collect his or her thoughts and write them down. One at a time, each member can then share his or her reflections on the process. Others listen until everyone has shared their reflections. This process provides space to ensure that people are comfortable with what has been decided and provides opportunity for the group to learn about itself. These matters are taken up in more detail in the next chapter.

5

Creating the Conditions for Group Learning

During a collaborative inquiry, ideas are expressed, heard, challenged, and agreed upon. This sounds like what happens in any group meeting. However, the purpose of collaborative inquiry is the generation of valid new knowledge and meaning that emerges out of an authentic process of collaboration and inquiry, through cycles of action and reflection. Successfully meeting this task requires the development of a group culture that facilitates learning.

GROUP LEARNING CULTURES

A rich literature exists on group dynamics and group process. The focus of this literature has, until recently, been on the impact of these dynamics and processes on task accomplishment and the satisfaction levels of participants. Only recently have researchers turned their attention to what processes influence the ability of groups to learn and the dynamics of collaborative learning (Dechant, Marsick, & Kasl, 1993; Imel & Tisdell, 1996). Kasl, Marsick, and Dechant (1997) have presented data on group learning that suggests that healthy group dynamics and group process are necessary but not sufficient conditions for group learning. They identify learning conditions that enable a group or team to learn by being supportive of what they identify as group-learning processes of Framing, Reframing, Experimenting, Crossing Boundaries, and Integrating perspectives. Armstrong and Yarbrough (1996) argue for the importance of the environment or group context for group learning, linking various dimensions of the internal and external group environment to the development of a group's capacity for learning. Brooks (1994) has investigated the impact of power on the production of new knowledge in organizational teams and concluded that power differences inhibit the production of new knowledge. Tisdell (1993) has described how the positioning of participants in the larger social structure impacts on power relationships within a group, influencing in turn the learning processes of the group.

Taken together, these studies present a complex and interdependent relationship between group process as commonly discussed in the literature, group-learning processes, and the production of knowledge within groups. Perhaps the most important factor differentiating learning groups from traditional task groups is the *explicit intentionality* of learning. In collaborative inquiry, this intentionality is carried to its logical conclusion—learning and the production of knowledge is the task. The criteria presented in Table 5.1, which we developed and used as a living group constitution, not only defined the parameters of our collaborative inquiry, but helped to provide a structure for the development of a learning group culture.

Developing a group-learning culture is critical because collaborative inquiry rests on the principle that experiences of individual members become the content for group action and reflection—individual learning both informs and is informed by group learning. At the beginning of our project on how learning is experienced in CI, we were not certain that there was such a thing as group learning. Like many adult educators, some of us considered the term *group learning* to be an oxymoron—individuals learn, not groups. However, as our project continued we came to experience two kinds of group learning. First, we came to recognize the power of the group for fostering certain kinds of knowledge construction. One member of thINQ observed:

> More and more I see how I learn better in groups. That I can only learn certain things in groups. Hearing words, or hearing phrases from other people, triggers certain things that make me think about something in another way . . . deepens what I'm thinking . . . without that . . . I kind of slog along. (thINQ, 1991-1993, p. 2363)

As our inquiry progressed, we became increasingly aware of the phenomenon of "porosity" as the basis for knowledge tacitly shared among the members of the group. Information and understanding were

developing in a nonlinear fashion. We learned to avoid premature conclusions. It may be a function of group learning that there are several
simultaneous currents of thought, ebbing and flowing, rising to the surface, or lurking at oceanic depths. We accepted the fact that ideas were
"floating in the air," that we had created them and had "based our work"
on them but hadn't "named them" yet. However, these ideas did exist
(thINQ, 1991-1993, p. 2885). When recognition of this tacit knowing
surfaced, we were surprised and delighted. Markers of this aspect of
group learning were the various synchronous "ahas" we experienced as
a group. These markers became part of the group culture and deepened
our reservoir of pooled knowledge. We came to trust the meandering
and chaotic nature of collaborative inquiry. Over time we recognized
that our shared stories, comments, agonies, and satisfactions had become the basis for a group culture. We came to recognize that each
collaborative inquiry group can be understood as a discrete, living
organism, capable of growth and decline. Like people, the group has to
cultivate a capacity for learning.

PRACTICAL ELEMENTS OF A
LEARNING GROUP CULTURE

The literature suggests that learning cultures are based on a foundation
of good group dynamics and power equalization (Imel, 1996). This
foundation supports at least three conditions of group learning. The first
condition is appreciation of teamwork, the openness of members to
hearing and considering other's ideas and the extent to which they act in
ways that help members build on their synergy. Second is individual
expression, the extent to which members give input to the group's direction and operations and feel comfortable expressing their objections in
meetings. Third are the operating principles that characterize the group.
These principles represent the extent to which the group has organized
itself for effective operation and has established a set of commonly held
beliefs, values, and purpose (Kasl, Marsick, & Dechant, 1997). Whether
these conditions are viewed as extensions of group dynamics or a subset
of group dynamics related to learning, they are descriptions of conditions characteristic of groups that learn—the conceptualizations of
group-learning processes. We turn now to the question of what actions
and practices establish these conditions of a learning-oriented culture in
a collaborative inquiry group.

Agreeing on Criteria That Define the Group:
A Constitution for Collaboration

During the initial informational meeting(s), the discussion has to involve expectations of how the group will function. These expectations are part of the basis for people making a commitment. Once people have committed, it is important that these expectations become codified, making explicit any assumptions people hold regarding group membership. One way of accomplishing this codification is to engage in an "I assume" session. With the definition of a collaborative inquiry group in front of them, the members take time for silent reflection and then write down completions for the statement "I assume that . . ." For example, "I assume that everyone is committed to attending every session." Each person can write down as many assumptions as come to his or her mind. The group then goes through continuous rounds of each participant stating an assumption until all assumptions are recorded on a board or an easel. Participants proceed to discuss, edit, and refine them into criteria that the group will use as ground rules for working together—defining characteristics of how the inquiry group will function to which all group members consensually agree to adhere. Alternatively, the participants may wish to engage in brainstorming as a method for surfacing assumptions and statements about how they will function as a group. The brainstorming list is then revised into criteria.

In our own inquiries, we have arrived at the criteria in Table 5.1 for structuring a collaborative inquiry group. As a way of thinking about these criteria, we have come to use the metaphor of "a group constitution," subject to interpretation, enforcement, and amendment, based on the needs of the group. Other groups may choose to modify or add to them—because, as we have repeatedly stated, collaborative inquiry is not a tightly proscribed process. The members of each collaborative inquiry need to agree consensually on, and commit to, those criteria that define *them* as an inquiry. The criteria should be consistent with the basic definition and spirit of collaborative inquiry as presented in Chapter 1.

The establishment of a learning-oriented culture begins with the definition of the criteria that members of group establish for their inquiry. These criteria can be seen as providing the initial operating principles of the group. The process of establishing them begins the appreciation of teamwork and individual expression. However, more specific group features and practices foster the development of a learning culture in

TABLE 5.1   The Criteria Defining Our Inquiry

Criteria	Description/Explanation
1. Inquiry is more than intellectual exercise; inquiry leads to action that is then reflected upon.	Reflection leads to action, or experience, and once again to reflection, a recurring cycle.
2. The purpose is to make new meaning.	This aspect presupposed that each inquirer has a store of information and experience, which serves as a resource for finding knowledge.
3. New meaning is generated "with" and "for" people; each inquirer is a participant, not a research subject.	Collaborative inquiry assumes that people are self-determining. Doing meaningful research with others is accomplished when the action and reflection are also self-directed.
4. The inquiry is holistic in its methods, not reductionistic.	Learning emerges from activity that produces it. The focus on learning through experience is the full context of that experience.
5. All inquirers are on equal terms in addressing the question, which sets up "a level playing field."	While some members of the group will have knowledge about certain issues, or more education or status, all inquirers are equal contributors.
6. All inquirers have the power to act on the question or issue being researched.	The ability of each inquiry to engage in the project ensures full involvement. All are capable of action and reflection on the issue.
7. Each inquirer is responsible for his/her own learning.	Each inquirer participates actively in the actions and reflections; this is consistent with the adult education principle that holds that learners are involved in the learning process.
8. Dialogue is the foundational aspect of the inquiry.	Dialogue honors the total process of learning and researching, not just cognition.
9. Participation is voluntary.	If participants are to take responsibility of their own learning, the learning context must be free from coercion.
10. Commitment to the group and its process is essential for the duration of the inquiry.	Episodic participation undermines the process. The group is a living entity that cannot function fully without its various parts.

collaborative inquiry groups—specifically, action and reflection, keeping reflective records, group ownership of ideas, collective or shared leadership and proper facilitation of group dynamics, and honest questioning.

Repeating Action and Reflection

At the heart of collaborative inquiry is the assumption that learning resides in the experience of the inquirers. The definition of collaborative inquiry presumes that an inquiry will be undertaken by people able and willing to take action and reflect on their experiences. Reason (personal communication, 1992) suggests that there is a dialectical tension between action and reflection that keeps the process of collaborative inquiry in motion. This dialectic implies a more complex level of awareness of the relationship between action and reflection than suggested in some of the seminal and more popularly understood learning style models incorporating cycles of action and reflection (Honey & Mumford, 1989; Kolb, 1984). As suggested in Chapter 1, action and reflection are discrete, but not necessarily polar, operations. Mezirow (1991) suggests that thinking can be considered an action—as when one draws on prior knowledge and frames of reference to undertake thoughtful action. Certainly engaging in dialogue and meaning-making within the group is a form of action. For Mezirow, thinking and introspection differ from reflection in that reflection involves a process of validity testing of prior knowledge or learning as one tries to understand a new experience for which past knowledge is proving inadequate or not assumed to be valid. Mezirow's ideas are important because various collaborative inquiry groups sometimes place limitations on how they understand action.

Action can occur outside the group between meetings and involve specific agreed-upon behavior. It can also occur inside the group as it works together. For some inquiry questions this form of action is the primary type of action taken. In the intuition group (Zelman, 1995), a series of exercises were conducted at each of the meetings; these exercises, incorporating the use of the senses in various ways, served as catalysts for reflection. In the teachers group (Bray, 1995), actions were taken outside of the group and then discussed when the group reconvened. In one technology integration group meeting, members gave brief presentations about technology initiatives they were spearheading. After they shared their stories, the group reflected on the actions each person took in his or her practice setting. Dialogues sparked deep levels of questioning by group members that precipitated further actions. In some sense, the group functioned as a support structure for members who were "pushing the envelope" in integrating technology in the workplace.

In both groups, reflection is needed not only on the action taken, but on the reflection process itself. Collaborative inquiry presumes this deeper form of reflection-on-reflection. During a meeting in April, 1992, Reason commented to us that

> being an inquiry group ideally involves reflecting on how that inquiry is going. . . . An inquiry group that is really working well is both looking at its inquiry process and the issues that it is trying to look at, and it is also looking at how it is doing that. How well it is doing that. So they go into that second level, that I think Chris Argyris talks about as . . . double loop learning: Reflection on reflection seems to be a key part of a good inquiry. (thINQ, 1991-1993, p. 684)

This higher level of reflexivity can be thought of as reflecting-on-reflection. It is a reflexive move that allows the co-researchers to examine their own processes of making meaning, consider how they are in relationship to the inquiry question, or, in the words of Steier (1991), tell a story about themselves. This process builds a culture of group learning and enhances validity of the group's conclusions. Researchers in many diverse fields are beginning to call for this kind of reflexivity that involves having researchers reflect on their own process and how it impacts their understanding. As a collaborative reflexive process, this is one of the most powerful aspects of CI as a learning and research practice.

As an inquiry matures, participants are working toward a capacity for reflection on three levels. At one level practitioners strive to develop enhanced capacity for reflection-in-action, which Reason has characterized as to "act with awareness" (thINQ, 1991-1993, p. 667). This includes, but is more than, cognitive awareness. Torbert (1991) describes it as acting with both conscious intention and holistic awareness, allowing cognitive reframing to occur in the midst of action. At a second level, they reflect back on the action taken relative to the question. This is coupled with taking the third, higher level involving the reflexive move described above.

Regardless of how groups structure their actions, there must be a balance between action and conscious efforts at reflection. Reflection, especially group reflection, can be a difficult and threatening process. We have noticed in our groups a relationship between fear of conflict and the inhibition of reflection. There needs to be an atmosphere in which conflicting ideas are encouraged and each person's contribution is considered vital and relevant. Later in this chapter, we will discuss the art of questioning, an important aspect of collaborative reflection. If the group adopts a friendly way of *challenging and provoking* in an atmosphere of trust, it will be enriched by expanded reflective possibilities.

As our group learning culture emerged, so did understanding of how reflection and action interrelate with each other. Reflecting individually and then together produced new ideas. We found ourselves repeatedly investigating and analyzing some ideas that took shape over a long period of time. Sometimes early reflections were significant but were dropped in the heat of discussion; we were often surprised to find, months later, that our earlier observations were significant. Sometimes these ideas would resurface in our deliberations. We rediscovered them by listening to the audiotapes of our meetings or referring to transcripts of these tapes. Continued sequences of action and reflection often served to enhance our appreciation of an earlier passing thought.

Particularly dramatic were those times when long-held tacit knowledge emerged verbally. We named those moments, especially when they were simultaneously arrived at by several people in the group, "Aha!" moments. The collective and almost visible nature of these moments made them powerful and memorable. Learning achieved in these moments did not become submerged again, but became part of our common lore and culture.

It may be fruitless to try to differentiate between the modes of action and reflection. For us, the distinction between action and reflection came to be accepted as fluid or "porous." Though uncomfortable with this idea at first, we felt more at ease with the concept once Peter Reason described the action and reflection process as starting to "pour into one another" (thINQ, 1991-1993, p. 724). However, inquirers should be vigilant that the periods of action and reflection remain in balance. While we have emphasized reflection as the mechanism for learning from action, it is action that triggers the learning, providing grist for the reflective process. Engaging in what Rowan (1981) describes as *Encountering*—putting plans and design into practice—is as critical as reflection in meaningful collaborative inquiry. In the absence of taking action, collaborative inquiry cannot lead to the mark of true collaborative inquiry—change in the participants, the situation, or both

(P. Reason, personal communication, 1992). To paraphrase Freire (1990), reflection without action is mere verbalism.

Collaborative inquiry is experienced as complex; some have described the feeling of participating in an inquiry as "being thoroughly immersed in a swirling process." In our own inquiry into learning, some of the seeds of ideas were consciously planted; others seemed to be borne by the wind. We experienced learning as a circular, spiraling, and meandering process, through recursive procedures of action and reflection. In the teachers group, one participant described the experience as "a process that weaves and turns and even after the meeting, I have reflected more than I do during the meeting" (Bray, 1995, p. 219). (See Box 1.1, in Chapter 1 for summaries of the inquiries referred to in this chapter.) Another participant, who thought that the element of surprise in the inquiry made the process exciting, added that the process "led to a growing, sort of webbing-effect where ideas come out of directions that we could never anticipate—That's a process of becoming" (Bray, 1995, p. 219).

A participant in the technology integration group drew a picture to illustrate how collaborative inquiry was experienced (Figure 5.1). Explaining her drawing, she wrote:

> In my drawing I pictured the beginning of our meetings with each person in the group as having bright ideas—those are represented by those light bulbs. People also had stellar ideas and those are represented by the question marks. These symbols represented a variety of points of view. These things are circled; they became more similar with new ideas being added at other points as the discussion went around and around, becoming more focused. The sense of unity became stronger at the end as this line demonstrates—it starts out dotted and then becomes solid and thicker. The thinking gets stronger and then it gets solid and whole. (Gerdau, 1995, p. 212)

Keeping Reflective Records

Another aspect of building a learning-group culture is finding inclusive solutions to issues concerning the inquiry process. Capturing experience and keeping records is an important part of the process—records provide the basis for analysis and meaning-making. However, since inquiry groups will typically embody a variety of personal learning styles, it is important to develop diverse methods of keeping reflective records. Each method must work effectively for the individual while

Figure 5.1. Imagination of CI Group Unity Becoming Stronger

meeting the needs of the group for accurate and comprehensive records of its experience. In our inquiry into learning, we each kept records according to personal preference or learning style. One member preferred putting pieces of paper on a bulletin board, and another had a ring on which she kept note cards. She kept this device in her bag and jotted down ideas and experiences as they occurred. Some of us wrote in narrative style in notebooks or on computers. Although these methods varied, they shared one thing in common—they provided the important records needed for our project, tracking our thinking and changes over time.

We also audiotaped every meeting and had the tapes transcribed. These tapes, embodying thousands of pages, served as an important "memory bank." Much of what we learned about ourselves as learners in collaborative inquiry came from studying this record and reflecting on it. As we returned to our collected narratives again and again, we were astonished to find kernels of an idea in places long forgotten. Our narrative texts provided fertile soil for ideas that evolved slowly, ideas that once seemed significant and were then abandoned, and convictions that needed gestation before full growth was possible.

Although we adopted the practice of audiotaping our inquiry sessions, other groups have used different methods of recording their experience. The methods used need to be consistent with the style of the group and the nature of the inquiry question. The community women's group adopted the practice of recording concepts that arose during sessions on large sheets of newsprint. The women also maintained journals by talking into tape recorders. These records became the basis for insights and themes as subsequent reflection and analysis revealed recurring observations and comments.

Some groups have asked that one person at each session serve as a "recorder," taking notes as the meeting proceeds. While this may prove effective for some inquiries, especially if the person playing this role is able to record comments on a laptop, it can also hinder the participation of the recorder. The members of the intuition group, for example, felt that taking notes inhibited their participation in the group's discussion (Zelman, 1995).

Whatever methods are adopted, it is important that appropriate records be maintained. They provide the foundation for reflection and for validating memories of past dialogue and experience.

Respecting Group Ownership of Ideas

An important feature of the collaborative inquiry process that must become an embedded value in the learning culture of the group is group ownership of ideas. This is not as easy as it sounds because it flies in the face of academic convention that values primary authorship and converts claims on seminal concepts into trophies of scholarship.

Early in our deliberations together, we found that we were trying to keep track of who said what. It became apparent that ideas emerged from varying depths of thinking and interchanges of ideas in ways that made attributing a specific idea to a particular person impossible. Worse, it raised the specter of interpersonal competition for attribution and the possibility that people might withhold ideas from the group rather than contribute them for further revision.

Paradoxically, the cultural value of collective ownership of ideas fosters a respect for others' thinking and tenaciousness on the part of the people advocating their perspectives. A corollary of group ownership of ideas is the need for each member of the group to feel that his or her voice is reflected in the findings or conclusions of the group. This is quite the opposite of what happens in task or decision-making groups in which collective responsibility means no one is responsible. In learning groups, everyone feels accountable for the meaning promulgated by the inquiry. Different positions are explored in dialogue in order to arrive at a common perspective that accurately reflects the experience of all. This is not seeking compromise. That would be unacceptable for groups seeking to construct valid knowledge. Rather, it is a process of seeking to discover the underlying basis for disparate experiences and different lines of vision leading to different interpretations and naming them. Each inquirer needs to be aware of his or her voice. Every inquirer has a unique form of expression; inquiry groups should value these voices as contributing to and enriching the articulation of collective findings.

An important aspect of collective ownership of ideas is learning how to let go of one's ideas. Sometimes a member of the group whose perspective is not resonating with the others will decide to "let go." How one decides to let go of a particular perspective is a complicated process. We have learned to "let go" because we came to realize that letting go is not "giving up." If the issue under discussion is critical to our future direction and we cannot reach agreement on the point, we postpone the issue, tabling it for future discussion. Sometimes this is done subtly through changing the topic or taking a break. Other times, it is done with formal agreement. We have learned that if an idea is important, it will come around again in our discussions after subsequent experience and dialogue have created a perspective that makes its importance clear to all of us. An important factor in helping us learn to let go is the lack of ego posturing in our group. One has to be willing to have one's ego work on behalf of the group, not one's self.

Developing a value around collective ownership of ideas requires explicit discussion among the members of the group. We surfaced the question of collective ownership of ideas early in our work. Together, we found ourselves citing each other in memos and working papers. Much later, while talking about it as an important element of collaborative inquiry as we were preparing a chapter for publication (Group for Collaborative Inquiry, thINQ, 1994), we came to realize how important this had been for our subsequent dynamics as a learning group. It was during this reflection that we discovered the importance of letting go that had became part of the tacit learning culture of the group.

Developing Collective Leadership

Just as important to a culture of group learning as collective ownership of ideas is the practice of shared collective leadership. If leadership is viewed as embedded in the person of a particular individual, then
collaborative inquiry is a "leaderless" group. However, from the perspective of leadership functions, collaborative inquiry functions under
conditions of collective leadership, with leadership functions distributed among the members of the group. It is our belief that this is fundamental to the development of a learning-group culture in which every
member is equal relative to the inquiry question. It is also fundamental
to ensuring that issues of power do not intrude on and inhibit the development of knowledge as some researchers have found happens in
learning groups (Imel, 1996). Social structural factors known to be associated with power issues in groups, such as social positioning and gender (Cahoon, 1996; Tisdell, 1993), can easily slip into the inquiry
process through the designation of formal, permanent leaders.

Leadership issues in collaborative inquiry are tightly linked with initi
ation and facilitation. As noted in Chapter 4, the responsibility for leadership rests squarely on the shoulders of the initiators or co-initiators
more heavily at the outset of group initiation and formation. As the
group moves into forming the question and designing the project, the
initiator must be sensitive to behaving in a way that does not communicate assumed leadership of the group. He or she must also be attentive to
nonverbal gestures that suggest the group is assuming a permanent leadership role on the initiator's part. In most cases the initiator must specifically address the leadership issue so that participants may negotiate and
contract regarding mutual roles and responsibilities. Most likely, group
members will have had experience with more traditional leader-led
learning and project management models so they may come to see this
initially as abdication on the part of the initiator.

For example, at the outset of collaboration, one of the members of the
technology integration group was taken aback by the idea of a leaderless group (Gerdau, 1995). Fearing frequent clashes and free-for-alls—
chaotic sessions that might prove personally uncomfortable—he was
concerned that the initiator might be abdicating responsibility too early
in the process, and he expressed alarm. Two other members of the group
stated their support for a democratic structure, and the issue was tabled.
The ensuing productivity of subsequent meetings demonstrated that the
group was capable of managing itself, and the apprehension evaporated.

Like other new or unfamiliar concepts, the idea of co-participation—research with people—is not easily grasped. Perhaps new metaphors are needed to communicate the essence of shared leadership in collaborative inquiry. The group might be viewed as a complex thinking organism, with each member a sensory receptor, responding differently to different stimuli but equally concerned with the survival of the entity.

This process of shared leadership can be initiated through an open discussion of the leadership needs of groups. Each person needs to accept the obligation of participating fully in shaping the direction of the inquiry and be open and frank about any doubts he or she might have at any point. This obligation of full participation can be maintained by each member openly expressing his or her agreement with decisions about actions or interpretation of the group's experience. The assumption that silence is agreement should not be a group norm—agreement must always be overtly tested.

Other leadership needs center around organization. An agenda for meetings needs to be established and shared with members before each meeting or generated at its start. Arrangements for facilities need to be made. Although facilitation styles can vary greatly, someone needs to pay attention to time and, when necessary, initiate a change in the agenda to reflect new time constraints. Channels of communication need to be maintained among members during and between meetings. Someone should pay extra attention to group process during meetings.

We have always rotated the leadership role, with each member taking a turn fulfilling it for a meeting. Within these broad parameters, the group as a whole needs to monitor and take responsibility for the process.

We cannot emphasize enough the role of reflective inquirers as one of the defining characteristics of collaborative inquiry. In our experience, this role is more difficult to adopt than it appears. It is especially important for individuals who are initiators of a collaborative inquiry *and for those who are accustomed to positions of responsibility and authority* to think through the implications and consequences of the co-inquirer role. Once the group gets under way, the role of "coequal" may be a difficult one for people accustomed to being leaders. It is important that the leadership issues be discussed openly.

The experience of role conflict. It is very easy for the initiator to experience a role conflict. He or she should be prepared for the possibility that the learning generated during the process may take the inquiry in directions other than those earlier envisioned. In the intuition group, the original question was greatly modified, changing the emphasis of the inquiry from the classroom to the individuals in the inquiry (Zelman, 1995). The focus and the direction of the inquiry changed; it was now inquirer-directed, not initiator-directed. As a co-inquirer, the initiator has the right—and the obligation—to influence this evolutionary process, but should not exercise ownership over the question or the direction taken. In fact, trying to exert leadership control will close off the initiator (or any other member of the group trying to exert control) from learning.

In seeking to avoid controlling the group, the initiator may overcompensate, leading to another form of role conflict. The initiator may hold back from participating fully, fearful that his or her participation will reinforce a tendency toward group dependency. In practice, each inquirer will vary in the degree of directiveness he or she brings to the group. The goal is to have full participation and all members, including the initiator, free to intervene in the group's process.

William Torbert challenged us to be interventionists within groups that we initiated:

> In my view you are inevitably an interventionist and observer, and that's just another way of saying what action inquiry is saying, that there's no way not to be both an observer and an intervener. . . . The more you're quiet the more weird it will seem to the group about why you aren't being a leader, right? And so there's no safe place in this. (thINQ, 1991-1993, p. 2535)

Torbert notes that in withholding leadership and facilitation, we would be demonstrating negative behavior. We could not expect others in such groups to become empowered if we were to disempower ourselves! He continued, "All you're modeling is powerlessness if you don't intervene, so the way to empower, is to be powerful, but also to inquire, test the effects of your power and invite other people in—don't cut off other people's attempts to initiate" (thINQ, 1991-1993, p. 2536).

Leadership through modeling behavior. Initiators need to be aware that the other inquirers may be waiting for them to model involvement in the inquiry process. This raises an important, often understated aspect of leadership. Even as a co-participant, the initiator has a responsibility to demonstrate through words and actions the behavior modes of collaborative inquiry, by gently encouraging participation by reticent participants, by actively eliciting divergent thoughts—as well as by, occasionally, remaining silent so to allow others to generate ideas. Often, it is the other participants who serve as models for collaborative inquiry. For example, in the teachers group there was not a single instance of absence throughout the inquiry. On one occasion, one woman's son had been ill all week. The meeting convened with her in attendance. When asked if her son was still ill, she said that he was, adding, "We made a commitment and I felt that if one person missed, we couldn't meet; we weren't the whole group" (Bray, 1995, p. 212). A similar sentiment was expressed by a member of the university learning organization group who stated, "This has precedence over other meetings" (University Group transcript, p. 351).

How the group feels about the levels of participation should be discussed openly and at regular intervals. The movement toward and achievement of an appropriate balance in participation is one of the biggest challenges facing an initiator. Early in the process the group will have a need to rely on the initiator for insight into collaborative inquiry. This should be kept separate from the inquiry question itself. As we remind the groups we participate in, we have some experience in collaborative inquiry, but are one of equals regarding the inquiry question. The goal, of course, is to get group members comfortable with the inquiry process and to learn from the uniqueness that characterizes each group. One of the worst assumptions that any initiator can make is that *this* group will be just like the previous one.

Questioning Honestly

Central to the notion of learning, and hence a learning culture, is questioning—not seeking definitive closure, but pursuing new paths and seeking new perspectives. Questioning is also a way of relating to one another, of challenging held perspective schemes, and probing for evidence and alternative meaning. Questioning should be considered a natural and integral component of an inquiry. Some participants may need to develop a tolerance for being challenged.

In our inquiries, we accept and value the art of questioning and the role it plays in learning. It has many benefits. To name a few:

- It dignifies our sense of wonder; it is invitational.

- It helps us to better articulate our thoughts; it generates additional questions that in turn generates better questions.

- It assists us in managing tension; it fosters critical thinking and critical reflection.

- It forces us to test the validity of our research conclusions.

For example, by their fifth meeting the technology integration group began to re-evaluate the intellectual soundness of its original question. One participant suggested, "Maybe the end really becomes not how do we get technology into the classroom, but what is the meaning of technology in classroom" (Gerdau, 1995, p. 202).

In the teachers group, several members were affected by the openness of the questioning process in the inquiry. One person stated that the more the group talked, "the more it makes me question my own teaching practices and a lot of the things I used to assume" (Bray, 1995, p. 217). His questioning of his perspectives stemmed from the inquiry's rational discourse and critical reflection. He revealed, "Every time I listen to group members talk, I change my mind. I have changed my mind about eight times here today" (Bray, 1995, p. 216).

The above comment reflects the cultural element involved. It is not just the behavioral act of questioning one another, but when the questioning becomes internalized each participant questions his or her own assumptions. That is the marker of a learning-group culture.

Practicing Reflection and Dialogue

As suggested in Chapter 4, periodic breaks for reflection on process issues, such as how the group feels about how leadership is being handled, are a powerful practice for facilitating group learning. One method for doing this is to hold a reflection and dialogue session at the end of each meeting, a practice utilized in other forms of learning groups (Dennis, Cederholm, & Yorks, 1996; Yorks, O'Neil, Marsick, Nilson, & Kolodny, 1996). Each member of the group can take a few minutes to reflect on how

- he or she would rate the group's process, and why,

- how he or she would rate his or her own participation, and why, and

- how he or she would assess how well the group is attending to leadership issues, and why.

If the group wishes, it can use either a numerical scale (1 to 5, for example) or a verbal scale (*needs improvement* to *very good*) to benchmark one's thinking, but the important data are narrative. Each member explains his or her reflection to the group without rebuttal or discussion, until every member has spoken. Then the group can have a more general dialogue and decide on what, if any, changes the group wishes to make in its process. This kind of practice enables the group to learn about its own process and facilitates the development of a learning-group culture.

THE IMPORTANCE OF A LEARNING CULTURE

The distinguishing characteristic of a collaborative inquiry group is its commitment to fostering learning. Accomplishing this requires the cultivation of a learning-group culture. We know from both the research findings of others and our own experience that this doesn't happen automatically. Many, perhaps even most, groups, including highly effective task groups, do not learn particularly well or fail to foster learning on the part of others. Developing a learning culture is an important goal during the early phases of a collaborative inquiry group—maintaining it an ongoing goal for the life of the group.

This is done as the group formulates its question, designs its project, and goes through the cycles of action and reflection. Paying attention to the practices highlighted above can lay the foundation for a culture of group learning. We turn now to the primary purpose of collaborative inquiry—making meaning for the group and communicating in the public arena. In doing so, we will also address strategies for enhancing the inquiry.

6

Making Meaning and Constructing Knowledge

This chapter focuses on the central challenge of the collaborative inquiry process—making sense of experiential data. Constructing new meaning through exploration, research, and individual and group change is the prime concern of collaborative inquiry. We use the terms *making meaning* and *making sense* interchangeably. For Reason (1988b, p. 8), making sense answers the question, "How can I understand what I have been through?" Making meaning, a term associated with Mezirow's (1991) theory of transformative learning, is "to construe or interpret experience—in other words, to give it coherence" (p. 4). The meaning-making process involves interpretation, analysis, reflection, and contemplation.

There is a distinction between internal meaning-making, in which the group pursues the answer to its inquiry question, and the making of meaning for the public arena, in which the group presents its findings to the public in seminars and in writing. Yet there is a strong connection between the two. We have found that periodically preparing to present ideas to a public audience enhances the meaning-making process by engaging the group in a rigorous level of reflective writing that brings clarity to emergent themes and provides for ongoing markers of the group's learning.

The practice of collaborative inquiry allows for creative interplay between the question and the methods used to answer it. These methods are highly experiential, inviting participants to draw on their sense perceptions and emotional reactions, as well as their cognitive capabilities.

This interplay presents opportunities for enhancing the inquiry process. It is also necessary to pay attention to the complex dynamics that often surface during the inquiry process to enhance the learning.

THE MEANING-MAKING PROCESS

Collaborative inquiry is not a linear process. In our work we have found meaning emerging even as we engaged in the early stages of planning the inquiry, during the cycles of action and reflection, and as part of an extended period of making meaning from our experience. As described in the earlier chapters, collaborative inquiry is an open process that seeks answers to questions that have no preset answers. It is a discovery-oriented form of inquiry, not a confirming or validating one. Meaning arises and submerges, is tacit and articulated, and deals with data one moment and the means of gathering data the next. In brief, change is a constant element in collaborative meaning-making. Periods of clarity are followed by confusion and then by more clarity. We never know where the inquiry will take us; we must constantly be mindful of its emerging nature.

Learning and meaning-making are inextricably intertwined. Mezirow's (1991) definition of learning explains this connectedness. Learning is

always involving making a new experience explicit and schematizing, appropriating, and acting upon it. We seek validation when, in the process interpreting an experience, we find reason to question truth, appropriateness, or authenticity of either a newly expressed or implied idea or one acquired through prior learning. It is important to recognize how crucial the validation of knowledge is to the learning process in adults. (p. 11)

In collaborative inquiry, learning from experience takes place both inside and outside the group throughout the duration of the inquiry group's existence, not just at the conclusion. At times, members may begin to engage in critical reflection, a process of examining their underlying assumptions and the activities that generated them. Group meaning-making is at the heart of collaborative inquiry. Collaborative meaning-making is valuable for two reasons: First, it results in enriched insights as participants share their experiences and provide diverse interpretations of what they hear from others; second, it can provide for powerful validity checks on the interpretations gleaned from these experiences.

Making sense is the process in which the group, through analysis and reflection, reviews its experience for knowledge and meaning. Meaning-making is contextually sensitive. In all forms of research, inquirers choose a method consistent with the type of question to which they seek answers. This is also true in collaborative inquiry. The questions to be answered determine how the inquirers look for them.

Meaning-making is an ongoing process. As the group goes through repeated cycles of action and reflection, nascent meaning emerges and is further tested, with new meaning continually emerging from the process. The group may not resolve the inquiry question during the time frame agreed upon. In this case, group members may agree to continue the inquiry beyond the originally agreed-upon time frame, building on the meaning that emerged during the inquiry. This may or may not involve the group reconstituting itself. At the conclusion of agreed-upon cycles of action and reflection, the group may set aside an extensive period of time for making meaning of their entire experience.

CAPTURING THE GROUP'S EXPERIENCE

Proper documentation is the basis for the meaning-making process. In Chapter 5, we raised the issue of reflective records. These records provide the data—in the form of narratives, presentational illustrations, and reflective observations—that are the objectified basis for making interpretative meaning. The methods for preserving experience need to be explicitly addressed at the beginning of the inquiry, although additional methods or modifications may be made as the inquiry unfolds. There must be a documented trail of experience that provides the database or text for learning from the experience.

There are a number of possibilities for capturing the lived experience of the inquiry, many of which are discussed in Chapter 5. Audiotape is an effective method for capturing dialogue during meetings, providing an ongoing narrative record of the inquiry. It is less intrusive or intimidating than videotaping, although for some inquiries videotaping is more appropriate. Videotape is especially valuable if a visual record of nonverbal behavior and movement is relevant to the inquiry question.

Transcribing audiotapes is a tedious process, and it can be expensive if done commercially, but the transcripts provide easy access to the group's proceedings. In the transcripts of our inquiries, we have numbered each line to facilitate the location and checking of text by others and ourselves. The original tapes need to be carefully dated and stored. It is impossible to over-emphasize the importance of careful cataloging and storage of tapes and transcripts. The open nature of the inquiry process makes it almost impossible to identify data or meetings sequentially without dated transcripts.

Transcripts and even audiotapes often do not convey the tone of the meeting. For example, at times we remembered things as more tense than was apparent from the tapes when they were replayed, leading to useful reflection on *why* we recalled an event as we did. For this reason, it is helpful for participants to take personal notes during the meetings for future reference. These notes should record critical incidents or encounters and how the person was reacting and feeling during these times. This often provides a personal context for the narrative record. These notes can be included in the person's learning journal.

Learning journals and notes provide documentation of specific transactions, events, and reflective observations. These are particularly important records of events and reflections on actions taken outside of the group context. The format of the journal should reflect the learning style and the needs of the participant. In terms of content, journals typically consist of descriptions of critical events and the person's reaction to them, as well as reflections on the event. It is important to note in one's journal what events have captured his or her attention or evoked strong feelings and emotions (Cell, 1984). Particular attention should be paid to feelings of incoherence (Culbert, 1974) when one experiences a divergence of reactions, either in one's self or from others. These become the grist for systematic reflection, first individually when recorded in the journal, and later collectively in the group.

Maintaining learning journals, like keeping thorough and accurate field notes in ethnography, requires commitment and discipline. The university learning organization group discovered how difficult it is to maintain the discipline of keeping journals. At the beginning of the third meeting, one of the participants observed that she hadn't taken the time to reflect in her journal. She commented on how faculty become upset when students don't complete their reflective assignments and wondered about what her failure to maintain her journal implied for her own teaching. Her own experience held implications for her reactions to students.

Drawings, schematics, mind-maps, and other forms of visual documentation can be very valuable ways of capturing experience. Poetry can be very evocative in capturing the feeling of a moment. The creative aspect of documenting experience is to free one's self from reliance on solely propositional knowledge, but documenting presentational and experiential knowing as it emerges from the experience as well. The systematic capturing of and reflection on these forms of knowing is one of the distinguishing characteristics of collaborative inquiry. In working with these various kinds of documentation, collaborative inquiry truly develops qualitative methods as in making meaning around the quality of human experience. This is a significant difference from merely utilizing verbal narrative in a way that mimics quantitative methods.

Working with the qualitative forms of capturing experience discussed above does not necessarily exclude any use of quantitative measures of experience. Many participants in collaborative inquiry have used learning style (Honey & Mumford, 1989; Kolb, 1984) inventories to assess styles and initiate dialogue in the group about their implications. Other groups have used the popular Myers-Briggs inventory in a similar way. Torbert (1991) has used indices that measure levels of individual development among participants. In some situations, the question may involve the impact of actions on quantitative measures such as student achievement scores or grades, response levels from clients, or satisfaction levels.

The important point when using such measures is that they are simply *measures* and should not be confused with notions of objective reality. All measures are operational definitions derived from abstract constructs that originate in either some form of observation and experience or the pregiven life-world. Qualitative experience is given priority over measures. When discrepancy occurs between experience and quantitative measures, it should be reflected upon, with a critical eye turned to the assumptions underlying the measure as well as the experience. The value of this critical reflection is found not in rejecting one or the other, but in learning through gaining insight into the source of the divergence. When using measures of learning styles and developmental levels and the like, care should be taken not to create categories that stereotype people.

UNDERSTANDING THE EXPERIENCE

The form of analysis adopted by the group depends on the question and how it is to be answered. Usually this will involve some form of inductive analysis, although a group may adopt a closed or pre-determined coding method as part of its work. Inductive analysis begins with open coding—the process of interpreting data and experience through developing themes or categories that communicate the patterns and meaning found in the documentation.

Devising a Methodology for Synthesizing Experience From a Spectrum of Methods

There are a spectrum of methods that can be employed in the meaning-making process, depending on the question and the interests of the participants. At one end of the spectrum lies storytelling around the experiences of the participants. At the other end is the practice of developing phenomenological themes and the practice of what we call phenomenology-in-several-voices. In between lie practices such as dialogue, reflection, and the use of metaphors. For example, in practice, groups may use a combination of these methods in exploring their questions, mixing storytelling with dialogue and reflection.

Storytelling

Storytelling is perhaps the most overlooked method in the human sciences, yet it is basic to how most behavioral scientists work. Before there are constructs and theories, application of comparative methods, and the development of analytical themes, there are stories. These stories are dutifully recorded in field notes and on tape recorders, eventually to be transformed into abstractions. A very lively exchange between Dyer and Wilkins and Eisenhardt around the development of case studies in research appeared in the *Academy of Management Review* (Dyer & Wilkins, 1991; Eisenhardt, 1989, 1991). Although the principal point that emerged from the exchange in terms of traditional research methodology was the need for rigor (Eisenhardt, 1991), another equally compelling point is evident in the exchange—regardless of methodological paradigms the beginning point of qualitative research is the story.

In collaborative inquiry, the starting point for meaning-making is typically the stories of experiences of the participants. These are listened to for trends, for themes, and for insights triggered in others. The secret of using stories in collaborative inquiry lies in using the timing of the story growing out of recent action, and using the comparative stories of others to help avoid the major limitation of stories often cited by traditional researchers—cognitive bias (Nisbett & Ross, 1980). At the same time, the strength of collaborative inquiry is building on lived experience, not secondhand experience. The participants are striving to avoid the discrepancy the wife of noted Harvard psychiatrist Robert Coles called to his attention early in his career, after listening to him present "learned" papers on young polio patients. To Coles' irritation and later edification, she could no longer endure in silence "what she called the 'discrepancy' between 'those kids as I know them' and 'those kids as you speak about them to your colleagues' " (Coles, 1989, p. 27). Using the various other methods described in this chapter, including questioning, careful reflection, and close attention to validity concerns, the group gains meaningful and carefully warranted lessons around its question. Collaborative inquiry places researchers in a position to "do justice" to their experience, rather than simply making reference to it in the course of offering abstract explanations.

Reason (1994a) states that collaborative inquiry "relies primarily on rational verbal reports of experience, but is branching out into imaginative storytelling and the use of metaphor" (p. 334). Our experience tells us this is an important aspect of the process. In the midst of our inquiry into learning, we found ourselves trying to identify the learning we had acquired to that date for a paper we were writing for a research conference (thINQ, 1993). Such writing for the public arena, we have found, brings a rigor to the reflection process, consolidates learning, and creates markers for group culture. We spent hours talking but made little progress. We changed strategies and began to tell stories about our experience in thINQ. To break the pattern of our thinking, we used an interview technique, holding an imaginary microphone, prompting one another with questions. This redirected our thinking, and from the stories there emerged themes that illustrated our learning at that time.

Storytelling is a particularly valuable practice when working with groups that are either diverse in terms of literacy skills or otherwise disinclined to spend time writing and analyzing. The community women used storytelling throughout their collaborative inquiry. Starting their sessions with a round of storytelling often surfaced themes, such as crossing cultures in their work or supporting one another, that led to more specific dialogue. The initiator recorded key phrases on newsprint for later reflection by the group.

While storytelling can initiate the meaning-making process, producing narratives of people's experience, it also provides markers of learning. In the process of telling the story, people realize they have acquired a tacit knowledge about things that previously they would not have been able to articulate. For example, during our dissertation work in May 1992, Linda relayed that on her train ride from Washington, D.C., to our meeting in New York, she had talked of our research with a businessman she met. She found herself concisely explaining the purpose and value of our collaborative inquiry in ways that she had not been able to express before. She recognized this experience to be a marker of her learning. Her story triggered two other members of our group to share stories that involved communicating with others—in a concise way—about collaborative inquiry. Afterward, we discussed how this may be an example of when something becomes knowable: an intuitive thing becomes articulated. This led to further dialogue about how talking with the businessman involved taking a leap of ownership of the research that she hadn't had before—that she had to "run the risk of inviting questions . . . and that happened . . . and I could defend my position and ask him about his ideas. We had a dialogue with new ideas" (thINQ transcript, May 1992, pp. 795-796).

Dialogue

Dialogue is becoming increasingly popular as a method for exploring meaning and for facilitating learning in a number of settings (Bohm, 1996; Isaacs, 1993; Schein, 1993). It is one of the principal methods of collaborative inquiry. Isaacs defines dialogue as "a discipline of collective thinking and inquiry, a process for transforming the quality of conversation and, in particular, the thinking that lies beneath it" (p. 25).

Dialogue requires careful, active listening with each party, not thinking about rebuttal but concentrating on what is being said, considering the whole person who is speaking, and being very conscious of one's reactions to what is said. Isaacs refers to this last practice as "listening to your listening" (p. 35). Speakers must be willing to explore the assumptions and structures of thinking inherent in their statements. The purpose of dialogue is not to rush to conclusions or to immediately influence others, but to share, understand, and assess the validity of the thinking of group members. Restraint is made possible by the understanding that everyone will have an opportunity to participate.

Habermas refers to this kind of dialogue as discourse. Mezirow (1995) describes discourse as "an effort to set aside bias, prejudice, and personal concerns and to do our best to be open and objective in presenting and assessing reasons and reviewing the evidence and arguments for and against the . . . assertion to arrive at a consensus" (p. 53). Dialogue, or discourse, is interconnected with critical reflection. "When we critically reflect on assumptions . . . and arrive at a newly transformed way of knowing, believing, or feeling, we need to validate the assertions we make based upon these transformative insights through this process of discourse" (Mezirow, 1995, p. 53). Careful dialogue around the experience is an important source of validity, an issue addressed in more detail below.

Mezirow (1991, pp. 77-78) specifies the conditions for rational discourse (or dialogue) as:

- accurate as possible information,

- freedom from coercion,

- openness to alternative perspectives,

- a desire to be critically reflective upon presuppositions and assumptions (including those that may be the basis for self-deception),

- equal opportunity for participation, and

- willingness to accept informed consensus as a measure of validity.

When dialogues are taped and transcribed, it is possible to reflect on what was said, paying careful attention to the words chosen for expression to the public arena.

One can quickly see how the conditions for effective dialogue and the criteria we chose for operationalizing collaborative inquiry parallel each other. It also makes clear collaborative inquiry's usefulness as an adult learning strategy. Following Mezirow, we hold that one of the most important functions of the adult educator is to develop environments that strive to minimize the distortions introduced by power and influence (both personal and structural) and ensure that all may fully and freely participate in the inquiry process. The model of collaborative inquiry is consistent with this function, even neutralizing the influence of adult educators by making them co-inquirers, subject to the same group learning norms.

Dialogue is the opposite of debate or heated discussion, in which the object is to defeat an opponent's views. It also bears an interesting relationship to consensus. Initially, dialogue should be practiced with the intention of forestalling consensus. Consensus should be reached only after thorough exploration of possible modifications of underlying patterns of meaning. The question of consensus will be discussed further below. Feelings of rejection that occur when one's ideas are not validated by the group, or reactions to having one's suppositions held up to critical testing, or emotions brought into the group from outside experiences and intensified by the group setting, can all lead to heated arguments instead of dispassionate dialogue.

Reflection

Reflection is an integral part of the meaning-making process. It is the basis for effective dialogue and validity testing. Heron (1988, pp. 49-50) identifies three forms of reflection. The first is *descriptive reflection*. During our collaborative inquiry meetings, members reflected upon their actions with regard to the inquiry question since the last meeting. Descriptions of events and responses to those events were shared among inquiry members. The object was to be as descriptive as possible, avoiding evaluative or interpretative statements. Heron (1988) labels this form of reflection "pure phenomenology" (p. 49).

The second form of reflection is *evaluative reflection*. This form of reflection ascertains the soundness of the descriptive reflection. Evaluative reflection embodies what Mezirow refers to as process reflection and premise reflection: "Process reflection involves both reflection and critique of how we are perceiving, thinking, judging, feeling, and acting. . . premise reflection involves awareness and critique of reasons why we have done so" (1991, p. 106). *Practical reflection* uses the other two forms of reflection to guide the future steps of the inquiry. This form of reflection applies previous learning to planning the next action experience of the inquirers.

All three forms of reflection take place during a typical collaborative inquiry meeting, usually following the above sequence. In our work we spent the early part of each meeting in descriptive reflection, each member sharing events that had taken place since our previous meeting. At the conclusion of each person's reflection, we would raise questions and engage in evaluative reflection. This evaluative reflection would often continue through much of the meeting. Practical reflection grew out of the evaluative reflection. As this process unfolded, individual members were reflecting-in-action (Schon, 1983) during the collaborative reflection of the meetings. It is the interplay between individual reflection and group reflection conducted through dialogue that produces meaning.

Other Modes of Expression—
Pictures, Metaphors, and Poetry

Meaning can find expression in pictures and metaphors that vividly represent the lived experience. In addition to asking questions, engaging in dialogue, and reflection, other methods exist for eliciting group learning. The technology integration group created visual representations of member's experience as part of its year-end reflection about what they had learned about collaborative inquiry. The results are both intriguing and compelling, and the drawings, along with the narrative explanations offered by the members, give "presentational voice" to many of our own experiences and were subsequently referenced by us.

One example of a metaphoric illustration follows (Figure 6.1). The person writes about her illustration:

> It is the structure that we were involved in that we brought our own separate entities into . . . and because it was this structure we were able to survive. These tiny circles that represent us are getting bigger and bigger and eventually they blend into almost a conglomerate shape. Now this is a box and when you bounce a ball into a box, what will happen? It will bounce out again . . . so hopefully, we will all jump out of this and carry with us our enlarged viewpoint. (Gerdau, 1995, p. 210)

From the beginning, we used the power of metaphor to communicate our learning to each other. Many metaphors were used to characterize aspects of collaborative inquiry, becoming meaningful artifacts of our group culture. One of the most important metaphors described collaborative inquiry as a "plaid"—a fabric woven of a variety of colored strands. Changing or removing one strand of color would entirely change the character of the plaid; likewise, changing any aspect of our collaboration would affect its essential character.

The intuition group, in addition to telling stories, experimented with other techniques for generating thought and discussion (Zelman, 1995). Usually part of each session was devoted to an exercise that involved sense perceptions. This exercise augmented whatever action occurred between the meetings. Some of the exercises involved word association

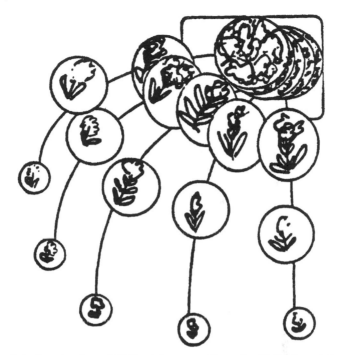

Figure 6.1. Imagination of CI Participants as Bouncing Balls Out of the Box
With Enlarged Meaning Perspectives.
SOURCE: Gerdau, 1995.

and "automatic writing," trying to "get to the unconscious." Some of the
participants were very "conscious" of their responses, yet the discussions evoked ideas about intuitive knowing. In one exercise, five repro-
ductions of paintings were brought in—works by Matisse and Magritte,
as well as ones by obscure painters. There were a wide variety of
responses to the works, with some people responding to color, others to
content, and still others to texture. The flow of the discussion that
ensued was typical of a style of exploration in which there was no
demand to answer a specific question; people pursued their immediate
lines of thinking and feeling. One of the participants described the discussion: "I feel that the way that I am able to talk about an experience
and think about intuition has very deep spiritual roots" (Intuition Group
Transcript, 1993, reported in Zelman, 1995, p. 364).

Poetry is another form of expression that can contribute to the meaning-making process. Robert Frost suggests that a poem is the "shortest emotional distance between two points." Laurel Richardson (1994), writing about the relationship between writing and inquiry, says:

> When we read or hear poetry, we are continually nudged into recognizing that the text has been constructed. But all texts are constructed—prose ones, too; therefore, poetry helps problematize reliability, validity, and "truth." . . . Setting words together in new configurations lets us hear, see, and feel the world in new dimensions. Poetry is thus a *practical* and *powerful* method for analyzing social worlds. (p. 522)

Poems can evoke both feeling and thought, linking the cognitive with the conative, translating tacit presentational and propositional knowing into explicit intentional statements of meaning. Because of this capacity for evoking both feeling and thinking, poems can serve to enhance communication of the experience to others. In doing so, poems and similar forms of expression link artistic knowing with empirical knowing through collaborative inquiry.

Constructing Knowledge

The purpose of these practices is to construct meaningful, practical knowledge. The most common way of expressing this knowledge is in the form of themes, capturing recurring, significant patterns that express the experience. Themes are usually expressed in narrative form (statements about the experience that has been validated through practices is discussed later in this chapter). There can be different strands of themes reflecting what happened, how it happened, and why it happened.

However, there are other, less conventional, ways of constructing knowledge. It can be expressed in subsequent action taken that reflects the new learning from the group, or the revision of policies. Teachers, for example, may alter how they structure their school's curriculum. Instructors may change how they approach their classes. These actions become the text that captures the learning. Such approaches to constructing knowledge reflect the assertion, made by Heron (1996) that practical knowing is the highest form of knowledge, transcending propositional knowledge. And, like the continuing subjection of propositional knowledge to future testing and revision, practical knowing must remain open to the lessons offered by new experience.

HERMENEUTIC PHENOMENOLOGY-IN-SEVERAL-VOICES

It is our belief that some of the most productive work in collaborative inquiry involves phenomenological description and hermeneutic approaches to interpreting lived experience, especially for those working to contribute to our body of knowledge in adult learning, education, community development, and organization development. Because of the complexity of the experience that we found in our work, the "chunking and sorting" of the qualitative methodologies were neither adequate nor appropriate for answering our questions. Our experience corroborates van Manen's (1990) claim that "meaning is multi-dimensional and multi-layered. . . it can never be grasped in a single definition" (p. 78).

Traditional qualitative methods have been well documented and are readily available in the literature (Creswell, 1998; Miles & Huberman, 1984; Strauss & Corbin, 1990). These methods can be adapted to some collaborative inquiry questions. However, the practitioner must be prepared to adapt them because they are presented in the context of traditional research assumptions; assumptions that the researchers, who are studying the experience of others, value propositional knowledge over all other forms and are maintaining distance between themselves and the objective of their study. We have found that the key to this adaptation of methods is adopting a posture of hermeneutic phenomenology toward the interpretation of one's own experience. It is this approach that we develop here, especially the development of phenomenological themes and the use of narrative language or writing. It was the use of these methods, first working individually, then followed by dialogue and discourse, that was the foundation for phenomenology-in-several-voices.

Phenomenological Themes

Van Manen (1990) distinguishes between themes in most qualitative research and phenomenological themes. In mainstream qualitative research, theme analysis is understood as an unambiguous and fairly mechanical application of a frequency count, the coding of selected categories in transcripts or texts, or some other breakdown of the content or protocol of documentary material. On the basis of these applications, computer programs have been developed that claim to do theme analysis for the researcher.

In hermeneutic phenomenological description, understanding the meaning of a lived experience is a process of insightful grasping and formulating a thematic understanding: not a rule-bound process but an act of "seeing" meaning (van Manen, 1990). A theme is the sense we are able to make of the phenomenon, the product of insightful discovery and disclosure. At best a theme is a distillation, but not necessarily a clarification. In our work, we adopted a phenomenological approach, returning to the experience itself, striving to recapture the experience *as it was experienced.*

The central method in this process was *bracketing*—the mental process of setting aside assumptions and concepts of coding in order to approach the experience, as much a possible, with a clear mind. Polkinghorne (1983) describes the process as follows:

> The method involves looking reflectively at an instance (or several instances) of the kind of experience under consideration. The instance (or instances) is then altered in imagination. This process of imaginative variation of altering allows for the shifting through of those aspects of the experience that are contingent and variable, thus leaving to be gleaned the necessary and sufficient ingredients—that is, the essence of the object of consciousness. (p. 42)

It is impossible for any researcher to completely bracket off his or her pre-interpretations. We all bring life concepts and values to each event. This view is taken by Heron (1992), who uses a phenomenological approach in developing his theory of personhood.

> There is a dialectical tension here between the bracketed concepts and the declaration. If you bracket the concepts absolutely out of the way then there is no determinate experience that you can identify and ask to reveal itself. If you don't bracket them off at all, the declaration is repressed by the conceptual imposition. So it's a compromise: you bracket off enough to get a declaration, but not so much as to make it impossible. This means the declaration you get is always relative to your bracketed concepts: There is no such thing as an absolutely pristine revelation of what the experience is really all about. (p. 9)

Heron's position is based on the hermeneutical phenomenology of Gadamer (1993), discussed in Chapter 2, that holds that there is no way we can avoid the history of our knowledge. Even the most revisionist thought is connected to cultural antecedents.

For example, in trying to understand how learning was experienced in our own group and in the other groups that we were working with, we strove to describe what was constant in our experience and what was variant. Based on our various group experiences, we generated a list of possible themes. This was accomplished by bracketing our theories and by describing the experience of participating in our field groups. While engaged in this process, we employed devil's advocacy and imaginative variation, trying to determine whether particular themes were essential or incidental to our experience. When someone offered a theme based on his or her perspectives, we examined it, played with the language, and determined whether it described the experiences of the rest of us.

A second method was the use of narrative language or writing. Phenomenological knowing is expressed in narrative—translating experiential, presentational, and propositional knowing held in one's head into text. This writing is descriptive, but because the description involves the use of language, it is also an act of interpretation. In writing, the dialectic between one's bracketed experience and the pre-given experience of the life-world contained in language becomes evident. Van Manen (1990) maintains that "hermeneutic phenomenological research is fundamentally a writing activity. Research and writing are aspects of one process." This assertion is not limited to hermeneutic phenomenology. Whyte (1991b), a traditional ethnologist and qualitative researcher, has observed that although "writing is not usually considered a component of research methods. . . it seems to me [to be] an indispensable part of the analysis process" (p. 270).

In our own inquiry, we would write as individuals, thematically describing our experiences with collaborative inquiry. In our group meetings, we shared our observations in the discourse of the continuing collaborative inquiry, collaboratively engaging in the mental experiments of checking the themes against our collective experiences. We came to call this process phenomenology-in-five-voices. Phenomenology-in-five-voices can be generalized to phenomenology-in-several-voices.

At times, we took a theme and worked on the language together, a process we refer to as collaborative phenomenology, the convergence of collaborative inquiry and hermeneutic phenomenology. We came to see a strong parallel between the cycles of action and reflection and the hermeneutic cycle of going from the whole—in this case the group experience of making meaning—to parts, or individual experience, and back to the whole group experience.

AVOIDING FLAWED MEANING

All serious inquiry must meet tests of validity. Regardless of one's philosophical leanings regarding the nature of knowing and the production of knowledge, "meeting tests of rigor is requisite for establishing trust in the outcomes of the inquiry" (Guba & Lincoln, 1981, p. 103). Ultimately, validity is linked to the question, "How do we know what we think we know?" The corollary to this question in terms of validity is, "How do we know we are not deceiving ourselves?" For one's audience, the question is, "On what basis should we accept your assertions or claims to know?" The inquirers must be concerned with avoiding self-deception and confirming the results of their work to others.

Collaborative inquiry is a special form of qualitative research (even if certain quantitative measures are part of the inquiry) closely akin to narrative investigation. Following Ricoeur (1971), the lived experience of the participants can be treated as a text to be interpreted. This text is found in the dialogues that take place and in the actions that constitute the history of the group. Polkinghorne (1988) believes that the concept of validity has changed in recent years: "It has become confused by the narrowing of the concept to refer to tests or measuring instruments. In narrative research, "valid" retains its ordinary meaning of wellgrounded and supportable" (p. 175).

Ricoeur (1971) introduces the notion of qualitative probability as the appropriate approach to validity in the context of hermeneutic phenomenology. He suggests that the logic of how interpretations may be tested is closer to the logic of probability than to the logic of empirical verification.

> To show that an interpretation is more probable in the light of what is known is something other than showing a conclusion is true . . . validation is not verification. Validation is an argumentative discipline. It is a logic of uncertainty and of qualitative probability. (p. 549)

In traditional qualitative research, the problem of validity is essentially a "question of whether the researcher sees what he or she thinks he or she sees" (Kirk & Miller, 1986, p. 21). The central concern of most qualitative research is whether access has been gained to the "insider's" world of meaning and action (Adler & Adler, 1987). In collaborative inquiry, the researcher has, by definition, access to the insider's world, with unique opportunities for validation through engaging in dialogue and phenomenology-in-several-voices—the question is whether the inquirer falls victim to collective self-deception. It is crucial that inquirers follow the advice given to traditional participant observers (Jorgensen, 1989) and document differences, disagreements, and conflicts among insiders (in this case themselves) on meanings relevant to the descriptions and themes that emerge.

Guarding Against Defensive Routines and Groupthink: Two Sources of Distortions in Group Meaning-Making

Two empirically based models have been advanced in the literature that demonstrate the ways in which group dynamics can unwittingly function to distort collective discourse in a way that produces invalid meaning: Argyris's defensive routines model (1985) and Janis's (1972, 1982) groupthink model. Both models assert the tendency for groups to become collectively fixated on a rigid frame of reference that predisposes their members to deny and distort both their inner and outer reality, a condition that Elmes and Gemmill (1990) have more broadly identified as a condition of group mindlessness.

The idea that group dynamics can interfere with the intellectual functioning of individual members has direct relevance for collaborative inquiry. The evidence around the defensive routines and groupthink models suggests that interpersonal dynamics may inhibit, or actually subvert, one of the supposed advantages of groups in decision-making and problem-solving situations—the ability to assess a situation from varied experience bases and forge more inclusive and objective solutions. Although the cycles of action and reflection that characterize collaborative inquiry are different from traditional situations of decision making and problem solving, the potential for group dynamics to subvert the critical thinking process within the group presents us with a potentially troubling phenomenon that might compromise the validity of an inquiry. This potential should deeply concern inquirers who are committed to avoiding self-deception and to achieving consensus around valid meaning.

Defensive routines can be defined as thoughts and actions used to protect the usual ways of dealing with reality among the members of the group. Within the context of collaborative inquiry, defensive routines can occur in two ways. The first has to do with group process and culture, as groups develop patterns of interpersonal interaction. The second way occurs when group members tacitly avoid challenging long-held assumptions that would reveal their experience in a different way. This different way of understanding their experience may be unappealing to members of the group in that it forces them to take personal accountability for dealing with their situation in a new way.

Essentially, defensive routines are adopted with a tacit acknowledgment by group members of situational factors that are problematic to the group but are considered to be either threatening or unchangeable. Defensive routines may be introduced into the group by individuals who are seeking to protect themselves from negative feedback or by persons trying to avoid uncomfortable confrontation or exposure to intense feelings. The group may collectively introduce such routines in response to the actions of one member out of fear that discussing the behavior will threaten the survival or future functioning of the group. Once adopted, both the routines and the phenomena the routines cope with become sacrosanct, beyond discussion. In a sense, they are functioning manifestations of the story about the "emperor's new clothes" in which none of the townspeople dares to tell the emperor that he is naked.

Examples of specific defensive routine behaviors include avoiding an issue by talking around it, withdrawing and perhaps engaging in gossip off line, and distancing by not accepting some responsibility for the situation. These behaviors invariably change what is permissible to discuss and result in not pursuing all aspects of the experience. Talking around the issue can take the form of people grousing about a situation, rather than either testing it through taking action or making a decision. In the community women's study, the action step of renegotiating the volunteer work contract with a county agency and working independently as a small organization, surfaced for months in the group's conversation. Instead of moving forward, comments like "Why won't the county listen?" and "How can we get them to understand what we do?" appeared and reappeared. Instead of examining the issue in terms of how they might test various attributions about their situation, the tone was one of rejection. The group physically looked crumpled, and would withdraw from the issue as a defense. Finally, on a hot August afternoon, the group confronted the fact that it had to make a decision about separating from the agency and test the appropriateness of their decision with action. Their body language changed, and the group moved quickly into planning proposals for private funding. Reflecting on both the community women's group and another inquiry done with the March of Dimes (see Box 6.1 at the end of the chapter for a summary of the March of

Dimes inquiry), Linda observed that defensive routines in both groups became more visible when there was a need for members to converge around themes from their divergent perspectives, to share the leadership roles, and to make group decisions.

Argyris (1985) argues that defensive routines are powerful and omnipresent within groups. These routines emerge without being taught or encouraged, and the most powerful ones emerge "where the intentions are honorable—namely, to increase the effectiveness" (p. 35). Defensive routines are counterproductive when they inhibit learning. Argyris uses the term "productive reasoning" to characterize actions that help surface and neutralize defensive routines (p. 262). He suggests that using productive reasoning "makes it less likely defensive routines will be created" (p. 262). Thus, he softens his earlier statements about the inevitability of their emergence. These are all useful as methods of guarding the validity of the sense or meaning made in collaborative inquiry.

Productive reasoning is characterized by the use of data that are accepted as valid by individuals with contradictory views. Here the value of the documentation becomes crucial, with people returning to data or text from live experience, as opposed to arguing over meaning and interpretation. Participants need to make explicit their premises and inferences, naming them as such, and identifying the data or warrant from which they are derived. Argyris and his colleagues (Argyris, Putnam, & Smith, 1985) write of reflection and experimentation as being at the heart of productive reasoning. This parallels in many respects Heron's (1985) and Reason and Rowan's (1981b) position of validity being enhanced through the repeated cycles of reflection and action. It also suggests the use of imaginative experimentation (Polkinghorne, 1983) that is part of the phenomenological method. Argyris suggests that defensive routines can be recognized and minimized through the use of open, reflective, and critical reflective inquiry. He acknowledges that this type of learning effort is very difficult in established groups with complex power relationships, varied personal interests among members, and entrenched defensive routines. This supports the need for periodically reflecting on the criteria defining a group's "constitution" (see Chapter 5) to ensure that these debilitating characteristics are not emerging in the group. It becomes easier to avoid the obstacles to productive reasoning and honest consensus if we recognize and acknowledge their existence as they emerge. To paraphrase Thomas Jefferson, "Eternal vigilance is the price of meaningful collaborative inquiry."

Groupthink as a threat to validity. Janis developed his groupthink model based on case study analysis of various public policy decisions, contrasting cases in which decisions turned out to be disastrous (e.g., Bay of Pigs), with a few that are widely regarded as successful (e.g., the Cuban missile crisis). In his original formulation, Janis (1972) defined groupthink as

> . . . a mode of thinking that people engage in when they are deeply involved in a cohesive in-group, when the members' striving for unanimity overrides their motivation to realistically appraise alternative courses of action. (p. 9)

Later, in response to criticism that his definition was too cumbersome and his discussion of the relationship between variables too vague (Longley & Pruitt, 1980), Janis (1982) offered a more structured five-stage model of groupthink as a decision-making process. In his new formulation, Janis defined groupthink as a tendency toward concurrence seeking. He continued to emphasize group cohesion as the primary antecedent condition for groupthink, and added a series of structural characteristics and factors relating to the decision-making context as additional antecedent conditions.

The structural characteristics relevant to collaborative inquiry are (a) insulation of the group, (b) a style of leadership that advocated a preferred solution, (c) lack of norms for using methodical procedures, and (d) social and ideological homogeneity of the group. The reader will quickly realize that the criteria defining collaborative inquiry are the opposite of these characteristics, again reinforcing their importance and the importance of diligence in maintaining their viability as characterizing the group.

Three remedies for groupthink are advanced by Janis (1972): (a) the use of devil's advocacy procedures, (b) developing alternative explanations for the data, and (c) being open to outside experts. These three strategies are also recommended by experts on qualitative research (Patton, 1990) and collaborative inquiry (Heron, 1988). Being open to responses from people outside the group is an important tactic for avoiding groupthink. In our own work, we have been very conscious of the need to be able to defend our work to outside audiences at conferences and in writing, not just for academic purposes, but to avoid becoming insulated and cut off from alternative thinking. Diversity in the group in terms of experience, gender, and learning styles can help participants avoid the advocacy of preferred solutions and the effects of social and ideological homogeneity. The reader will already realize that collaborative inquiry builds on creativity and even playfulness in methods, not being slavishly wedded to a particular methodological approach. What is important is the development of strong norms around pursuing a variety of methods and raising challenges to the validity of emergent meaning. The speech acts described in Fisher and Torbert's (1995) discussion of action inquiry are valuable tools for effective challenging of emerging meaning. Illustration and inquiry, on the part of those advocating a position, should follow advocacy. Otherwise advocacy becomes debate.

Checking Validity in Collaborative Inquiry

How, then, do participants in a collaborative inquiry know they have come nearer to some notion of truth? Establishing the validity of any inquiry is a process of identifying the threats to validity in the type of study being conducted and of developing a method for countering these threats. Above, we have discussed potential threats inherent in the collaborative process. Others will be situation-specific. We have also already mentioned some specific actions to help establish validity—devil's advocacy and being open to outside interpretations of experience.

We have found that the devil's advocacy process is facilitated by the cycles of divergence that emerged out of our writing and other actions between meetings. Heron (1985) has identified the cycles of divergence and convergence that accompany the cycles of action and reflection as an important part of the validation process, as have Reason and Rowan (1981b). In our experience, divergence provides the basis for inquirer triangulation, or collaborating our experience through the processes of phenomenology-in-several-voices and collaborative phenomenology. We use sources of collaborating experience from at least three people as the basis for considering a finding as being collectively valid.

We also utilize what can be considered method triangulation, by comparing different sources of documentation. Following Jick (1979), we expect to encounter some divergence in the sense of meaning produced by varied sources. Exploring this divergence led to richness in understanding and insight. When our actions involve encountering others, we can check our interpretation of the experience with them. We can also share findings with informed outsiders who can play devil's advocates.

Authenticity as a Warrant for Meaning and Knowledge

Lincoln and Guba (1986; see also Lincoln, 1990) have advanced another set of criteria appropriate for establishing the warrant for conclusions arrived at through collaborative inquiry—authenticity criteria. These criteria can be employed in addition to the methods discussed above or on their own. Lincoln and Guba developed the concept of authenticity as an alternative to the conventional language of validity. They offer four authenticity criteria. The first is *fairness*—does the record demonstrate that the viewpoints of participants have been given evenhanded representation? Demonstration that all parties participated as peers and without being intimidated through power relationships helps establish this criterion. Reflection around the governing ground rules of the inquiry helps to insure fairness. So does the reporting of minority positions along with the supporting arguments.

The second criterion is *ontological authenticity*—the extent to which there is evidence of increased awareness among the participants of the complexities of the issues surrounding the question. To what extent does the record demonstrate a growth in the perception of the participants? The third criterion is *educative authenticity*—the existence of evidence that participants have gained increased appreciation for the sources of alternative positions around the question. The final criterion is *catalytic authenticity*—accounts of the actions and decisions promoted by the inquiry process. This can be established through the demonstrated willingness of participants to be involved in change.

These criteria are especially useful in instances in which not all participants agree on interpretation of the experience. They are consistent with a phenomenological approach in that they allow the experience to speak for itself as opposed to reliance on methods to attest to the validity of the conclusions. In addition, the authenticity criteria speak to what Reason (1992) has described as the key marker of effective collaborative inquiry: that it produces change in the participants and/or their context.

COMMITTING TO THE INQUIRY AS A LIVING AND LEARNING SOCIAL ORGANISM

Collaborative inquiry is a method that depends on holistic learning on the part of the members of the group. As the learning culture develops, the group *becomes the learning space* and must be nurtured as such. This involves at least two issues, celebrating meaningful collaboration and distress facilitation.

Celebrating Meaningful Collaboration

The more the participants appreciate each other as people beyond their role as group members, the better the inquiry. Empathic knowing among "whole persons" provides a strong foundation for the resolution of differences within the group. The group should create mechanisms that support the meaning-making process and allow time for empathic knowing to develop. Examples of such mechanisms are "check-ins" at the start of the meetings, periodic "time-outs" to assess what is really going on in the minds of the participants, and "debriefings" or "final reflections," in which people can interject their personal responses to the process at the close of the meetings.

Check-in refers to taking time at the beginning of meetings for people to share with the group what has been going on in their lives apart from the inquiry, how these events may or may not impact on their participation, and how they are feeling. Each person usually takes about 4 or 5 minutes for their check-in. We have had people come into meetings with the good news of an exciting opportunity at work, concern for uncertainty about job security, and health issues affecting either themselves or a close family member. This brief check-in brought each of us into the group as whole people and provided a context for others to understand what was going on in each other's lives. This is a much different experience than the more common one of coming into the room and dealing with an agenda, while other concerns and distractions may be flowing beneath the surface.

Time-outs allow for reflection on the process and give space for people to articulate "where they are" in the process. Final reflections or debriefings also allow for process reflection and bring public closure to the meeting. Both provide for learning on the part of the group.

Time spent socializing apart from the inquiry contributes to fuller participation within the inquiry. Given the time and energy busy adults will invest in collaborative inquiry, it is important for the group to celebrate its shared experience in whatever manner and at whatever time it deems appropriate. We found that many valuable insights or "truths" arose in a relaxed after-meeting atmosphere, watching a movie, having lunch, or just walking in the snow while on a pizza break. Away from the pressure of the meeting, free association and "what if" thinking provided breathing room. Humorous speeches, the exchange of inexpensive gifts, and eating dinner in a favorite restaurant are simple rituals any group can employ to express mutual gratitude and appreciation. Collaborative inquiry, like any other social context, provides an opportunity for people to extend their relationships beyond the boundaries of the group. Shared recreation during "free time" is important to the inquiry process, more fully revealing the whole person.

During the university learning organization inquiry, a serendipitous event facilitated resolution of the strain that existed between two of its members. The January meeting had to be postponed because of snow. It was going to be held at the home of one of the members involved in the strained relationship. The other person couldn't be reached with word of the meeting cancellation, and he arrived as scheduled. The two visited, talking for more than two hours, arriving at a much better understanding of each other's ideas. Later, one of them commented on how it was good to talk about a range of things and get to know each other as parents and as persons with a range of interests and concerns. This chance meeting provided a foundation for their relationship, and the tension between them never resurfaced.

About halfway through its inquiry process, the university learning organization group shifted its meetings from a conference room on campus to the nearby home of one of its members. The group would meet before the session and eat and share stories. The atmosphere was different, and people "saw" one another beyond their formal faculty and administrative roles. Following this switch, the inquiry deepened and became more focused.

Distress Facilitation

During the conduct of an inquiry, participants encounter one another's perspectives and there is bound to be an occasional clash of ideas. The stress generated should be dealt with directly and without delay. The pressing concern of having to move forward with the inquiry can inhibit the group's willingness to take the time to alleviate tensions. Individuals may carry their concerns outside of the group when their distress is ignored or glossed over, creating an unseen but damaging rift within the group. It is healthier emotionally to resolve interpersonal issues in the group before moving forward with task concerns. Addressed early, such issues are often easily resolved and the group can move on with its deliberations. However, if resentment lingers and is not brought into the open, long-held tensions that finally surface will not be as easily resolved.

The group may avoid discussion of distress because it is seen as a source of conflict rather than a source of learning. One member of a collaborative inquiry group expressed his insight into how interpersonal relationships and distress are related as follows:

> I felt uncomfortable with what was happening . . . there was an affective, "I did not like this." . . . Later on I started to ask myself the question, "Why did I not like this?" So, it's sort of like the affective generates the need, at some point in time, to go back and have additional reflection that says to me, at least in certain instances, learning is an upsetting process. . . . You've got to sometimes be upset if you're going to be able to learn . . . that can very easily lead to conflict, but I think . . . the two interact in some way that I'm not real clear about yet. The deeper the learning, maybe the more the unsettledness. (Interview transcript with participant, May 1994)

John Heron (1992) discusses the dynamics of distress so commonly found in the context of group process:

> A certain amount of distress emotion is enabling; it is a shock or spur to growth and development . . . the fear of the unknown can be a motive for learning and inquiry. Beyond a certain threshold of tolerance, distress ceases to be enabling, goes into overload and becomes disabling. (pp. 128-129)

It requires courage and processing skills to handle distress issues effectively. It also requires concern for and trust in the group.

Distress may emerge in the process because participants bring in previous experiences with groups that may lead to attributions about the behavior of others that, if not verbalized and checked, can create stress and distortions. In the university learning organization group, a tension emerged between two members of the group. During a discussion about classroom practices and standards, one of the two asked the other, "I noticed you seem to be talking to me a lot during the comments and so . . . I wanted to know if you were reacting to anything that I said?" The other member responded that she was not. Later the first person commented that "at some point I have to defend myself" to which the other said, "I didn't mean it as an attack." The first replied, "I felt attacked."

Some discussion of this followed before the group discussion became redirected.

After the meeting, it was clear that both participants wanted to discuss the subtle tension that seemed to underlie their relationship in the group. The ensuing discussion had a more relaxed and authentic quality about it than was true during the meeting. As the discussion continued, members of the group made the observation that Lyle, the initiator, had been quiet for much of the meeting and often sat with his head somewhat down. They interpreted this as a sign of disappointment on his part in how the inquiry was going. He said this was not the case; he was just concentrating on the discussion. This was a very valuable piece of feedback for Lyle, leading to recognition of how his body language was affecting the group. It also led to some critical reflection on his part, whether, if at some level, his body language was reflecting anxiety over the process.

Notes made about this post-meeting discussion state that the discussion "proceeded to a very direct conversation—comfortable, natural, reaffirming conversation" and that "it feels like we crossed a bridge in talking about process issues." The two were taking the first steps toward understanding how the other was reacting and the initiator gained valuable learning about his impact on the group.

There is a reciprocal relationship between defensive routines and distress facilitation. Confronting defensive routines, whether in regard to general group process or in the process of making shared meaning out of experience, initially heightens distress. Distress is often accompanied by heightened use of defensive routines. Defensive routines enable groups to avoid addressing distress, seeming to smooth over issues, but actually enabling it to continue. In the teacher's group, group members were almost universally gracious with one another. When distress occurred, members often did not discuss it, taking their distress out of the meeting and dealing with it by themselves. This is basically withholding behavior and represents a lack of trust in the group.

COMMUNICATING IN THE PUBLIC ARENA

Collaborative inquiry empowers participants through enabling them to learn and become more effective in their own arenas of practice. In our experience, many groups do not communicate their findings to the outside world. This has three important downsides. First, the body of knowledge generated remains unavailable to others. This unintentionally impoverishes fields such as adult education, in which the experiences of practitioners and their various constituencies should be part of the knowledge base that informs theory (Group for Collaborative Inquiry, 1993). Second, it cuts off the dialogue around what has been learned from challenge by others. Such critique from outside the group provides an important force for freeing the group from groupthink by allowing the members to examine the critique and either reject it or modify its conclusions. In either case, validity is enhanced. Third, as we have previously mentioned, the process of writing for the public arena helps the analysis or meaning-making process and provides a record of the group's thinking at particular points in time. For these reasons, communication with the larger public arena is an important part of the consensual meaning-making process.

Initially, we thought of the proposals, papers, and presentations we made as requiring compromises between the desire to continue generating new ideas and the need to construct a product. We designated these periods "task modes" and considered them a necessary nuisance, intrusions on our learning mode. Now we understand that these periods of articulating our experience forced us to review our learning and to reconfigure it in order to communicate with others in the field of adult learning. These encapsulations of our learning, painful and confining as they may have been, helped further the inquiry process, causing us to stop and assess its progress. Our initially "unwanted tasks" helped us see the learning being produced through collaborative inquiry.

Modes and Forms of Communicating Experience

The traditional form of communication is a written document—a paper, article, or book. Other relevant presentation opportunities include workshops, meetings, seminars, and faculty development contexts. Communication often happens in stages. At various points, collaborative inquirers will respond to "the task mode" and will need to generate interim reports of their work or consolidate their findings, however tentatively. Despite the pressure of deadlines and having to speed up the meaning-making process in order to meet the submission deadlines of conferences and publications, we came to recognize these activities as a significant part of the collaborative inquiry process. Committing words to paper is a very personal experience. So, too, is going public with a set of findings, regardless of the media used. The process of communicating outside the group raises the psychological "ante," fostering a more intense process of dialogue and reflection, and more careful consideration of the words and other symbols adopted. The quality of learning is the beneficiary of this intensity.

Perhaps the most daunting challenge we face in developing a useful guide to collaborative inquiry is to communicate the energy, the passion, the stress, and the fun of the experience. Time and space constraints, plus the limitations of the narrative form, often cause the distillation of meaning into a somewhat dry text (present example included). An audiotape or more theatrical presentation mode may add significantly in demonstrating the power of what was learned. As much as possible, the manner in which the meaning is communicated should be as multifaceted as the experience itself. We have enjoyed communicating the essence of collaborative inquiry through poetry as another way of communicating to others the experience of learning through collaborative inquiry. For example, John wrote "Rollercoaster."

To see what it was like, they ventured on the coaster
What an odd group of venturers.
Powered to the top by the hamsters in their wheels.
None had known what the ride would be.
Some believed that in their intellect
the ride would find meaning.
But as the train crested that designed rise,
they realized the ride would be more.
Yelling, screaming, vitalized they careened down the slope.
Being thrown for a loop drained their energy.
Outside and inside the car, they hurtled on.
Some thoughts went back to why,
others looked only at the second.
All else had departed their minds in the rush that enveloped them.
Some clung fiercely to each other,
some rode by themselves.
Eventually the end was in sight,
Eventually they stopped.
They asked if they could ride again.
In the days since that ride some have said that it
started at the crest,

others say it started at the ticket booth.
Having ridden the coaster, they are no longer what they once were.
(Bray, 1995, pp. 137-138)

The Conundrum of Who Communicates in the Public Arena

Ideally, communication to the public arena is seamlessly integrated into a collaborative inquiry group's process of understanding its experience. As suggested above, preparing to communicate facilitates the meaning-making process. Our collective communications as thINQ facilitated our understanding of our experience. Formulating these communications paralleled our other meaning-making episodes, sharing and capturing stories of the experience, engaging in dialogue around the commonalties and differences, and building consensus around what we were going to communicate. Once this consensus was formed, individuals or pairs might take pieces of the message, working to put it into form, either visual or narrative. The group as a whole reviewed its work, with collective modifications being made in the final product. We all participated in the presentations.

A conundrum emerges when some in the group do not wish to participate in the communication process, but are engaged in the inquiry for the personal learning. Similarly, some members of the group may not wish to communicate to certain audiences or may feel that the form of communication required by certain audiences will fail to represent the experience as they lived it. At the same time, the option of not communicating to the public arena may be distressing those members of the group who wish to avoid the loss of the group's voice about its experience as part of a larger dialogue around the question being explored by the inquiry.

There is no facile resolution of this dilemma. In part, these issues can be minimized by discussion of the important role that communication to the public arena can play, both for the group and for the larger community of interested persons, at the beginning of the inquiry. At minimum, if the members of the group do not wish the group's experience communicated, their wishes must be respected. This seems a basic tenet of research ethics even beyond acknowledgment that the experience is owned by the group. If the group agrees that members can report on the experience, other members should review any communication, a form of member check. In our experience, participating in collaborative inquiry heightens one's awareness of the distinction between one's individual voice and the voice of the group. Any group member must be careful about assuming the authority of the group voice.

CONCLUDING COMMENTS ON THE CONSENSUAL PROCESS

This chapter has discussed the methods for revealing meaning and identifying themes from a collaborative inquiry. It has also discussed issues surrounding validity and group dynamics.

Ultimately, the meaning generated is based on consensual validation. The consensual process first seeks input from all group members integrating the various viewpoints into the meaning produced; it is successful when all members are in agreement. A collaborative inquiry group, although composed of individual learners, develops into a learning organism. The consensus process gives tangible evidence that group learning is taking place.

Inquirers contribute a variety of possible interpretations during the meaning-making process. Achieving consensus compels the group to delve into the richness of interpretation in a manner not available to individual inquirers. Through the consensual validation process, more complex interpretations emerge. Our groups have been diverse in learning styles, gender, and areas of professional practice. Our collaborative inquiry experience has been that diversity creates tension *and* breadth of perspective.

For collaborative inquirers, consensus is a methodological issue because of its relation to validation and its integral role in the group-learning process. The consensus process should not lead to the "lowest common denominator" that members can agree on. Achieving consensus is not a series of tacit agreements; the collaborative inquiry group must be open in reaching decisions. Inquirers should not assume agreement by other group members. Group members must be vigilant to avoid premature closure, attempts at directive leadership prior to consensus, and assumed decisions. "Are we all agreed?" should be followed by a clear demonstration of agreement or disagreement by each of the group members. We always went around the group at these points. If consensus is not actively sought out and protected, the meaning-making process will be flawed.

It is important to take time to celebrate collaboration. True collaboration is often hard-won and tiring, but the results are rewarding. Having dinner together, taking a walk, and telling stories that recall significant events in the group's history are all forms of celebrating the time spent together. Group activity that recognizes the rewards of working together while taking a respite from the process of inquiry can bring many returns as the group remembers to appreciate one another as individuals.

BOX 6.1

The March of Dimes Inquiry

The March of Dimes Inquiry involves the use of collaborative inquiry to explore complex issues surrounding teen pregnancy and parent education. The inquiry began in 1993, when the director for a local March of Dimes in the Washington, D.C., region participated in a workshop led by Linda Smith and a colleague of hers, Beverly Spencer, who was coordinator of a community health program. The one-day session described developing a peer counseling service using the process of collaborative inquiry.

Immediately after the workshop the program director asked, "What's next?" Quickly Linda and Beverly set a meeting date. Over two dinner sessions, the three worked on a proposal to help the March of Dimes create a model for using CI to facilitate better program planning. The director believed that the inclusive process of collaborative inquiry would match current needs to expand community program services.

The invitation process stretched over three months as the three talked with many community organizations about exploring collaborative inquiry. Most of the program managers wanted to know exactly how CI worked and what kinds of outcome might be expected. As these discussions progressed, teen pregnancy surfaced as the topic around which considerable energy existed for inquiry. Ongoing media coverage, insufficient funds, and no easy solutions contributed to beliefs that the topic was compelling.

For the next 18 months, staff from 37 non-profits in the Washington, D.C., region worked with March of Dimes staff in collaborative inquiry groups initiated by Linda and Beverly to explore the complex issues surrounding teen pregnancy and parent education. A three-session workshop series held over nine weeks provided the basic structure for the March of Dimes project. There were two inquiry groups, meeting a few days apart in different places in the region. Both groups engaged in rounds of storytelling to discover more about what members wanted to examine and learn. Members agreed to audio- and video-taping to document the process, as well as capturing themes on large sheets of easel paper.

Important stories of services and management flowed quickly. The stories served as a greenhouse for the remainder of the inquiry. In one of the inquiries, a member suggested drawing a mural to make sense of the many ideas found in the group's stories, a method also adopted by the second group. In both groups, the murals reveal similar themes of common ground and current program gaps, a form of collaborative evaluation and needs assessment.

After creation of the mural, members of one group returned to the concept of an overarching question. They decided their inquiry question was, "How do we connect with teens to provide meaningful program services?" After developing this question, inquiry members carried out informal and formal activities linked to the question. Informally, they created smaller partnerships to share services and ideas. To communicate in the public arena, the group completed a handbook and a videotape that told the story of its collaborative inquiry.

7

Variations and Unanswered Questions

Peer learning in a community setting, university professors experimenting with their teaching, secondary teachers linked through Internet technology, exploring how to enhance their practice—very different settings and very different people all engaged in a common activity—all participating in collaborative inquiry. An important question emerges, however: What is the impact of these differences on the CI process?

In one respect, the answer to this question is somewhat disingenuous; collaborative inquiry is a very flexible inquiry process that is defined more by its epistemological assumptions than by any specific structure. Each collaborative inquiry group defines its process and adopts those methods most adaptable for exploring its question. In another respect, the question is critical, because by examining experience with differently structured collaborative inquiries we learn more about how CI can be applied in different settings to leverage learning.

INSIGHTS AND LESSONS FROM VARIATIONS IN APPLYING CI

Our understanding of how differences impact the collaborative inquiry process is still in its early stages. Generalizing from the number of cases available in the literature without more dialogue pursuing this kind of inquiry would be both reckless and counterproductive. Furthermore, it would be contradictory to engage in a mechanistic analysis of such an organic process. What is possible is the sharing of some of our reflections on those differences among inquiries that, in our experience, seem important for discussion. Three such lines of difference are (a) whether the inquiry is conceptualized as research or learning, (b) the creation of multiple groups for fostering systemic change, and (c) the role of technology in expanding the opportunities for collaborative inquiry.

Collaborative Inquiry Focused on
Research Versus Adult Learning

We have argued that collaborative inquiry is both a strategy for adult learning and a method for conducting research in the human sciences. In practice, collaborative inquirers place emphasis on one focus or the other, with implications for how the inquiry is conducted and experienced. At the core of these differences is whether participants are engaging in a collaborative inquiry for purposes of producing new meaning and knowledge just for their own learning or producing meaning and knowledge for the public arena.

The application of CI for the public arena encourages discourse among practitioners in terms of both content and the inquiry process, fostering advances in both areas. It also moves forward the agenda of opening up the research process in a way that counters distortions resulting from much conventional behavioral and social science that fails to reflect on its own historical situatedness. It also produces a rigor that enhances the learning process.

Conducting collaborative inquiry for the public arena requires multiple methods to help validate claims of learning, careful documentation allowing others to understand and follow the story of the inquiry, and a commitment on the part of participants to work together to communicate their experience in a compelling and accurate manner. When utilized in this way, each phase of the collaborative inquiry process engenders learning in and of itself along a number of dimensions. Practitioners come to have a deeper understanding of the limitations and potential of various research methods for producing meaning around the question of interest. There is an ongoing sense of discovery as the members of the inquiry confront the conventions of academic practice. This process of discovery is at times as frustrating as it is exciting. As the inquiry proceeds, inquirers often gain an enhanced appreciation for how deeply they have internalized the assumptions of their life-world, even when they think they have been critical of them.

The challenge to one's assumptions about research is especially true when the inquiry takes place within institutional settings such as graduate programs. In such settings, people repeatedly bump up against the institutional requirements and restrictions requiring repeated justification of the use of CI as a research methodology. In the process of confronting these conventions, participants inevitably reflect on their own motivations and goals and the question of whose interest the research is for. These pressures are in addition to the realization that the members of the group come with different understandings of the research process and the values of CI. The bottom line is that conducting CI in this context is a significant project that is labor-intensive and can span several years.

By contrast, collaborative inquiry applied to create meaning for the development of the participants is experienced primarily as an opportunity for learning. As an adult learning strategy, CI is experienced as an alternative system of knowledge production that has utility in the lives of the participants. The key is that it produces change in how participants view their world and function in it.

When applied in this way, CI tends to put special emphasis on oral tradition. When CI is employed primarily as an adult learning strategy, discourse and discussion on experience are considered research activities that are validated through future action. There is less emphasis on the need for codification, although we believe it is important for participants to document their experience in order to provide a foundation for future reflection on their experience. The tasks involved are equally intense, but somewhat different than in inquiry for the public arena. For example, record keeping may not require transcribing tapes to produce written transcripts; detailed meeting notes may suffice for process and content reflection. The sharing of experiences through storytelling or reporting on actions taken between meetings can be very intense as co-inquirers challenge one another's assumptions through questioning and capture themes on easel charts. The role of the adult educator, as co-researcher and learner, is to encourage the process in a way that enables the group to produce meaning that is trustworthy and has real utility in terms of the growth and development of the members.

More specifically, it is possible to differentiate between inquiries that place more emphasis on research and those that place more emphasis on participant learning in terms of three dimensions: the inquiry's purpose, the theoretical frameworks that provide its foundation, and the group culture that manifests itself. These three dimensions (purpose, foundational theories, and group culture) relate, respectively, to processes of generating knowledge and meaning, the use of human experience in the inquiry, and the group culture that evolves (see Table 7.1). The columns of Table 7.1 have a foreground/background relationship that transposes itself depending on whether the inquiry has a primary emphasis on research or adult learning. This reflects the porous relationship between the two foci, each of which is part of the same whole. The arrows are intended to imply movement or shifts between the two foci that may take place as an inquiry progresses. At times, an inquiry may move more toward a research focus as participants consider communicating with a particular public, and then move back to more of a learning focus as the participants focus more on their own needs for learning around the inquiry question. While such considerations may move the co-inquirers toward one focus over the other, the phenomenon of collaborative inquiry still contains both foci at the same time. This wholeness allows the group to relate learning and research in a multidimensional way, much like a gyroscope, to expand the potential for discovery. Most inquiries will tend more toward one focus or the other depending on the intention of the participants.

If the inquiry has a research emphasis, conducting formal analysis through explicit methodological practices becomes more salient. There are heightened concerns around building consensual knowledge and meaning in answering the inquiry question. Any communication to the public arena is likely to include discussion of methodological concerns.

Conversely, if participants are primarily concerned with their own learning and development, the focus is more centered around fostering individual and group insight. Developing the capacity of participants for directing their own learning becomes an important part of the inquiry. The various inquiries that provide the basis for this book represent this continuum of applications ranging from research in a university setting to discovering practical knowledge useful to participants in their own settings. Almost all of the inquiries varied at different points in time along the research/learning continuum as they unfolded.

Foundational theories relate to the credentialing of the methods used in the inquiry. They provide part of the answer to the question, "Why this approach to answering our question?" Participants in a collaborative inquiry with a research focus have to give more attention to the philosophical foundations for their claims to making knowledge as they forge their methodological practices. Their methods may be variants of phenomenology, hermeneutics, ethnography, or grounded theory.

TABLE 7.1 Research–Learning Continua in CI

CI Element	Research <div style="text-align:center">◄──────────────►</div> Learning	
Purpose in Generating Knowledge	• *Focus on* methodology for building consensual knowledge for the public arena	• *Focus on* developing skills, competencies and capacities within the group and among individual co-inquirers
Theoretical Foundations for Use of Human Experience	• Phenomenology • Ethnography • Grounded Theory Learning • Hermeneutics • Critical Theory Learning	• Experiental Learning • Trial and Error • Transformational • Action Learning • Action Reflection
Creation of and Working in a Group Culture	• *Uncovering assumptions* about research • *Trustworthiness*: What are the dynamics of testing what is valid? • *Identifying* the public arena, institutional/contextual scholar influences surrounding publication and presentation	• *Uncovering assumptions* about learning • *Trust*: How do we offer and receive learning from each other? • *Identifying* the private sphere, institutional/organizational team, or individual leadership factors or participants

Learning-focused inquiries are more likely to be guided by experimental trial-and-error learning, learning through experience, transformational learning, and action learning theory.

The focus of the inquiry obviously has an impact on the cultural values that take hold. In more research-focused inquiries, these values tend to emerge around the assumptions participants hold about research and the institutional contexts in which they expect to communicate. In learning-focused inquiries, these values reflect emerging assumptions about learning and settings in which participants are taking action.

Once again, these are not discrete categories but descriptions of how the nature of collaborative inquiry shifts back and forth depending on the focus of the inquiry.

Systemic Change: One Group Versus Several Groups

Collaborative inquiry groups commonly foster learning and change in individual inquirers. Extensions of the process are now being implemented in school settings for the purpose of producing learning and change at the group and organizational levels. These experiments involve groups of teachers who embark on their collaborative inquiries as part of the same initiative, but with the intention of generating a pool of knowledge that will impact the larger system of which they are a part.

Joyce initiated collaborative inquiry for professional development in Millburn Township public schools, a premiere K-12 school district in northern New Jersey. She introduced the four-phase framework of collaborative inquiry during Millburn's Staff Development Day in October 1997. From that point forward, regardless of grade-level teaching assignments or subject area specializations, teachers organized themselves into 15 collaborative inquiry groups. Membership in the groups coalesced around each group's interest in a compelling curriculum question grounded in everyday practice. One hundred teachers (approximately 40% of the teaching staff) volunteered to participate in the collaborative inquiry process. This approach to professional development represented a departure from the district's traditional staff development programs in which participants listened to presentations from outside consultants or attended one-day workshops.

Called "The Curriculum Commons Project," the initiative was supported through a competitive federal grant, Educate America: Goals 2000. Grant money subsidized the hiring of substitute teachers, provided laptop computers for curriculum development and classroom use, and enabled the district to purchase curriculum development software. The overarching aim of the Curriculum Commons Project was to support teachers in curriculum development project groups to become effective in the model of collaborative inquiry. This was for the purpose of advancing district initiatives around establishing a technological infrastructure for the development of an online curriculum. Additional purposes included introducing a constructivist approach to curriculum development informed by the results achieved by students, interacting with the broader educational community about curriculum development, and communicating the value of the Curriculum Commons experience.

The 15 groups devised inquiry questions driven by their common concerns. Examples are "How can we utilize the Internet to facilitate inclusion and mainstreaming?" "How can we use the Internet to teach, to stimulate interest, and to increase student productivity?" "How do we utilize our instructional resources to align an integrated, thematic, developmentally appropriate curriculum?" and "How can special area/ special education professionals communicate and share the value and content of their programs with general staff?"

All 15 CI groups met for 3 full days over the course of the academic year. As self-managing, leaderless groups, they took action on their questions between meetings, maintaining communication at formally scheduled face-to-face meetings, on telephone conference calls, and by e-mail. Then they reflected on their actions at subsequent meetings.

Perhaps incredibly, all of the groups answered their burning questions and framed solutions to the problems implicit in their questions. In addition, each group, as part of its meaning-making process, wrote a "Group Learning History" synthesizing their experiences as co-inquirers into a narrative describing what they learned, how they experienced learning together, and what actions they planned to take to improve educational practices in their classrooms or across the district. To satisfy the requirements of the grant, each participant completed a survey developed by an outside consultant, collecting data in 41 discrete categories measuring growth in teacher's collaborative capacities. Both the learning histories and the survey produced laudatory accounts of the experience. The specific outcomes are most appropriately discussed elsewhere. Collaborative inquiry proved to be an effective strategy for fostering professional development. The participating teachers created a pool of new knowledge and new meaning. This pool resulted in the development of a more dynamic curriculum, not to mention a more collaborative culture.

This application has several features of interest. First, it involves the potential constructive tension that can exist between CI and institutional needs. The project assumed a degree of alignment between the questions of practice development that would be pursued by teachers and the broader institutional goals. However, it required senior administrators to accept that inquiry would proceed along the lines of inquiry driven by the teacher's experience. Of necessity, this required their giving up bureaucratic control. This produced a little anxiety on the part of Joyce, the initiator, who was well aware of the potential for problems. She had to keep lines of communication open and reinforce the values of open inquiry.

Second, the project demonstrates the halfway ground that often exists between doing collaborative inquiry for the public arena and doing it to meet private needs (see discussion on communicating to the public arena in Chapter 6). The primary purpose of the inquiry groups was to address the needs of participants. However, it was also hoped that the participants would communicate their experience with others in the educational establishment.

Third, the design of the project demonstrates the potential for technology to expand the possibilities for the design of these kinds of inquiries, a topic to be given additional consideration below. The use of software and e-mail allowed the group to work effectively in between the grant supported meetings and to overcome physical separation.

The second application involves an extension of the work John did initially with his school district in rural, upstate New York. This, too, involves the use of CI as a substitute for conventional, expert driven, staff development days. Once again in 1997, John proposed to both the teachers and school administration the establishment of collaborative inquiry as an alternative to traditional in-service days. Three CI groups were formed, involving virtually all of the secondary teachers in the school. Each group met for the equivalent of three full days.

The questions reflect the diverse concerns of the members. One group organized around the question, "How can we improve the school culture?" Another group addressed the question, "How can we use technology more effectively in the classroom to promote student learning?" The third group, composed of the four members from the original CI group initiated by John several years ago, chose to continue with the question, "How can we improve our practice?" However, the focus of the third group evolved into a different direction than the members initially anticipated. Originally, they expected the group to focus on teaching strategies, but the inquiry turned into a focus on cross-curricular involvement among group members. This change seemed to be a reaction to the scattered, autonomous, subject-oriented approach to education that characterizes much of their practice today.

As with the Millburn effort, this is not the place to detail the learning that took place, but an assessment following the process provided compelling evidence that participants found the process to be both energizing and personally rewarding in terms of their learning. Additional evidence is found in their plan to continue their work in the coming year, with one group planning to meet during the summer months.

Both the efforts in Millburn and upstate New York have been successful in terms of teacher participation and learning. The question here is what lessons we can draw from the experience regarding multiple group initiatives with systemic change implications. Three lessons seem to be valuable to pass on to others. First, if properly initiated, groups can function responsibly without ongoing facilitation. Second, the largest source of tension is around the empowerment of participants to implement their action strategies. Third, the learning can be leveraged through cross-communication among CI groups, although this process must be fostered.

Independent Functioning of Groups

Although it will seem superfluous to some, there are several matters that must be attended to at each meeting. Ensuring that these matters do receive proper attention from the group usually requires one member of the group to commit to paying specific attention to them. This role can be rotated or played by a member of the group who the other members agree is best suited to play it.

The various dimensions of group process that need to be paid attention to have been discussed at length in previous chapters and are mentioned here again only for emphasis. These include ensuring that

- mechanisms for avoiding consensus collusion have been identified and are being employed (validity checks),
- consensus decisions are being overtly agreed to by everyone (no tacit approval),
- all members are being heard from and able to freely participate,
- high stress levels are recognized, and distress facilitation is used when necessary,
- action steps are clearly articulated, and
- members reflect on the process at the conclusion of each meeting to identify possible areas for improvement and check that the group is following its intended norms and procedures.

Even when the facilitation role is accepted by group members, the initiator of the CI process remains a resource for additional facilitation. When severe process difficulties arise, the groups usually seek the help of the initiator to provide them some guidance so the process can continue. Whether or not this is supposed to be so in the theoretical sense is one question, what is real is another. When involved in this way, the initiator should avoid giving specific direction or explicitly "siding" with some parties. Rather, he or she needs to make suggestions, offer observations, and ask questions that help the group's members to reflect on what is happening.

Tension Between the CI Groups as Self-Directed Learners and Institutional Control

When collaborative inquiry is pursued within institutional settings, the initiator can expect to play an ongoing role as the interface between the groups and institutional administrators. Normally, the initiator has negotiated the institutional "space" and support for the inquiry. This means he or she is perceived as having credibility with the institution.

Usually the institutional administrators have an expectation that since they are providing something the participants want (the opportunity to pursue CI), there must be something they can expect in return. It is important that shared interest in the importance of the questions being pursued and belief in the benefit of allowing people to engage in open inquiry be the basis of this social exchange. Initiators need to resist promises of specific returns-on-investment beyond the intrinsic value of the process itself and the importance of the questions being explored.

Institutional representatives do have a right to expect to receive reports on the learning. In instances where funding, release time, and other forms of support have been provided, the institution will likely require some form of assessment of the experience. Again, theory aside, the reality is that the initiator often has to negotiate an assessment process relevant to the CI process.

Here, the Millburn example provides guidance. The assessment was conducted on an action research model, with the initiator working closely with another researcher to craft a design that would not violate the basic assumptions of collaborative inquiry and treat participants as subjects (Gerdau-Lee & Davis, 1998). Such a design requires a relationship of dialogue with the participants, in which their voices provide the learning reported. The process needs to be as much as possible a form of reporting to the public arena, with any additional researchers playing a role of outside devil's advocate. There is undoubtedly an element of compromise in such an arrangement, and it falls on the initiator and the other participants to manage the process in a way that balances competing needs (theirs and the institutions). Exploring such accommodations is often necessary to allow CI to gain a foothold as a vehicle for establishing generative spaces for learning in institutional settings. In our work, we have been interested in learning more about how collaborative inquiry can be used in these settings in a way that establishes collaboration not only with the co-inquirers, but with the institutional contexts in which they are sometimes embedded.

John believes that as CI gets its legs under itself in a school system, there is a growing possibility that it will be used by teachers as a powerful systemic change agent. Because teachers seem to choose issues to research that are incredibly defensible in the public arena, they have more political clout than they imagine or are used to experiencing. Because the questions lead to actions that provide contextually sensitive answers for improving the learning environment for students, the inquiries produce conclusions that are enthusiastically supported by school administrators, boards of education, and the public. It is difficult to argue against well-thought-out proposals that are within the capability of teachers to implement. Theoretically, there may be difficulties for inquiry groups in implementing their actions in schools, but this situation has yet to evidence itself in our experience. At least in the case of John and Joyce's work in school systems, CI seemed to open up communication and visions of what it is like, not only in other classrooms but also throughout the system. Perhaps it can work in similar ways in other institutional settings.

Linda's work with the March of Dimes provides one suggestion that it can work in other institutional settings. (See Box 6.1 at the end of Chapter 6.) Her work also demonstrates the need for perseverance on the part of the initiator. Linda had to build support over a period of 3 months, visiting many affiliated organizations in the Washington, D.C., region. Her experience, however, is a model for how communicating to the public arena can involve participants directly in the assessment process without involvement of others.

Cross-Communication Among Groups (Sharing the Learning)

Our data demonstrate that participants experience CI as energizing. For example, teachers openly state that they are able to teach with more enthusiasm for weeks following a CI reflection session (Bray, 1995). Even when participants are experiencing burnout, collaborative inquiry seems to produce regeneration or reinvigoration (Bray, 1995; Gerdau,

1995; Smith, 1995; Yorks, 1995; Zelman, 1995). This energizing effect, combined with an immense curiosity about what other groups are doing, leads to informal sharing among groups about their learning. There is a practical side to this sharing as well. Participants within groups pursuing similar questions want to validate their learning in the experience of others and avoid "reinventing the wheel" in some of their methods.

When members in different collaborative inquiry groups work in the same organizational setting, a certain amount of sharing takes place naturally. This informal sharing can be formalized by creating more formal structures for communication among the groups. Periodic community meetings can be held, during which groups can listen to members describe their experience and engage in dialogue. Depending on the number of groups involved, the design for community meetings may vary.

If there are only four or five groups, one way of generating productive dialogue is by having each group participate in a fishbowl discussion among the members about their experiences, while the others listen. In a fishbowl, following a brief period of preparation, groups take turns having a 5- to 10-minute free-form conversation among themselves about what they have been learning. The rest of the community listens to their discussion. Their conversation is followed by a period of questions, comments, and dialogue from the listeners. While the general focus of the fishbowl discussion may be structured around general topics such as "What we are learning about" or "What general dilemmas we are facing?" the purpose of the fishbowl design is to stimulate people into new, spontaneous insight of tacit knowledge. The design is also more engaging than listening to formal presentations and reports.

In some instances, having groups dramatize their learning using short skits is another effective way of encouraging this kind of dialogue among groups. In a very different way, establishing a computer chatroom for participants can open up the flow among groups.

John's groups of secondary teachers are considering a federated design in which members from the various groups may interact with a core group, looking for linkages in the learning among the groups. The specifics of this design have not been worked out. However, the emergence of this idea from the participants in the various groups speaks to the desire to foster this kind of cross group learning. It also holds significant potential for influencing the culture of the school in a more dramatic way.

Using Technology to Expand,
Extend, and Enrich Collaboration

Our discussion in previous chapters has been limited to the application of collaborative inquiry in face-to-face situations that provide the psychological time and space for human relationships to form and grow. We are learning, however, that CI can also be conducted at a distance, either synchronously or asynchronously. One of the lessons of the Millburn experience is that group members can take full advantage of new technologies by communicating between meetings through e-mail or through online discussions. Internet search engines can be mined to locate information related to the inquiry question. Software for collaborative writing now exists so members of a group separated physically can still brainstorm, draft, edit, and publish a piece of collaborative writing, despite the distances that separate them.

"pcAnywhere" is a product that allows for inquirers to sit at their computers and take over a computer at another site. This enables information to be accessed more easily. In addition, if one person is having difficulty manipulating a software product, another user can actually use it while the first person watches his or her computer being used. "CU-CeeMe" (as in, see you-see me) software allows for videoconferencing. While this technology can enhance collaborative inquiry at a distance, our enthusiasm for technology is tempered by our belief that integration of technology into CI should not supplant the personal experience of collaborative inquiry. Face-to-face collaborative inquiry may be enhanced with collaborative inquiry at a distance, but we believe that there is no substitute for the face-to-face experience. The use of technology tends to keep people on task. In our inquiries, the times we were not on task, even sometimes far astray, seem to be the times that build the most meaningful bonds among co-inquirers. These bonds become critical in times of resolving divergent experiences and their interpretation, aggressive validity checking, and distress facilitation. Also, these periods often seem to precede very important insights. Understanding how these dynamics are influenced by technology is itself a topic for inquiry.

Furthermore, each technology restricts collaborative inquiry in some way. Text-based computer conferencing does not communicate facial expression and body language. Videoconferencing via satellite is a form of television production that can be prohibitive given the costs and time constraints involved. Desktop videoconferencing is a promising medium, but participants must have access to computers equipped with video capabilities and expensive videoconferencing software. Still, the use of technology is the next frontier of collaborative work (Schrage, 1989).

UNANSWERED QUESTIONS

Using collaborative inquiry primarily as a method of conducting research versus producing adult learning, initiating multiple groups to foster systemic change in organizational settings, and integrating technology into the CI process provides us with a peek at the future directions this approach to inquiry may take. We are just beginning to learn about the possibilities and the limitations of these variations. Our hope is that other inquirers will explore these options as part of their own journeys into CI and join us in dialogue around their experiences. We turn now to some other questions that need more research through collaborative inquiry. Our hope is that these questions will inspire other collaborative inquiries, especially among faculty and graduate students in disciplines related to adult learning and development.

How Do Task Requirements Influence Learning in an Inquiry Group?

One issue that we would like to learn more about is how external task requirements influence learning within groups. Our experience suggests that learning often follows twisting, meandering paths not limited to specific inquiry questions; this is a process that emerges as the group learns together. We considered the group's re-framing of its question as a true marker of group learning. Participants look beyond the initial inquiry question to confront other questions, learning about themselves, the process, institutional contexts, and a range of issues related to the primary question.

In thINQ, significant learning occurred during the "learning mode" —our free flowing discussions; learning also occurred during the "task mode" —when we were required to produce presentations of our understanding to others, in verbal or written form. During the task mode, we consolidated the learning that we could name at that point, fashioning it into communicative form. These instances, although considered a nuisance, were later to become mileposts of the inquiry. Although task requirements facilitated our learning, the dynamics of how this occurred and why it occurred are not clearly understood.

Some learning theories assert that working on meaningful tasks is an important aspect of personal and professional development. For example, as discussed in Chapter 3, Action Reflection Learning™ theory (O'Neil & Marsick, 1994) rests on the premise that professional development is best accomplished by having people work together on important tasks. As a strategy for implementing learning from experience, collaborative inquiry assumes that the inquiry question is meaningful for all participants in the group. The pursuit of this meaningful question can result in occasions when specific tasks have to be accomplished. If we are to use the process optimally, we need to know how task constraints influence and shape the learning experience in collaborative inquiry. Comparative work on the differences between self-imposed tasks, as in CI, and externally imposed tasks, as is sometimes the case in action learning programs, will contribute to theory development and practice in both learning strategies. Understanding the role that "learning modes" and "task modes" play in collaborative inquiry is an area for further investigation. Inquiry may help us determine when task demands are functional and when they are dysfunctional.

What Is the Impact of Role Differentiation in an Inquiry Group?

One of the areas of interest to some members of the learning organization group at the university was the idea that not everyone assumed the same role in the group. Nor did each participant carry out the same action assignment.

One example of this issue is the role of the senior academic officer. Given the demands placed on his time by the university system—demands that he could not influence, such as attendance at some administrative cabinet meetings—he could not attend every CI group meeting. After much discussion, the other group members agreed to include him in the inquiry despite this constraint. They made this decision to include him primarily because some members saw his continuing participation as important to their hopes for learning about and influencing the university as a learning system. Eventually, this person's role evolved into that of a resource providing the group with necessary information on the institution, helping the group to navigate through institutional constraints, and providing his perspective on some of its deliberations.

Similarly, the participants in this group did not have parallel action assignments. Because of their varied roles in the university, some worked more specifically with students; others assumed responsibility for implementing the learning communities cluster that was one of their action strategies. This contrasted with the other groups members of thINQ were working with, in which all members had the same action assignments or roles.

The potential impact of such role differentiation on inquiries is not well understood. Experience with other role variations is likely to produce valuable insights into how collaborative inquiry can be implemented in a variety of contexts.

How Does Context Influence an Inquiry Group?

Learning more about the importance of the institutional context is another area for inquiry. Our collaborative inquiry groups have taken place within contexts in which there was some support from high-level administrators. We have not explored the implications of initiating CI in a context lacking such support. Would CI take on more of the character of participatory action research effort, similar to those initiated by researchers grounded in critical theory? What would be the personal costs to the participants? How would the experience of learning be altered? What ethical questions would confront initiators?

Beyond the question of institutional support are questions regarding the broader institutional context, such as working in public versus private institutional settings. What additional complications arise in for-profit settings and settings dedicated to cost reduction, such as HMOs? We have already experienced the constraints that funding agencies can place on an inquiry. For example, the Millburn work had to submit to an outside assessment using conventional questionnaire methodology. Furthermore, the initiator had to write a report on the project. Both activities go beyond the epistemological assumptions of CI.

In her work with an organization in Washington, D.C., Linda had to deal with organizational constraints. She describes the March of Dimes as having more of a corporate than an institutional culture. A large, national organization that has accomplished its primary mission (a preventive vaccine for polio), it continues to seek another great mission that is as clear-cut as its first one. Much of the work that gets done at the March of Dimes is tacit, submerged, and carefully protected, much like changing corporate cultures.

Viewed from the perspective of a corporate culture concept, the challenge faced by Linda in her inquiry was one that occurs repeatedly in such settings—a change of leadership and the subsequent change in understanding and commitment. The person who had worked with Linda in initiating the inquiry advanced to another position, relocating to another geographic area. Another person took her place as a primary contact for Linda, and it took time to establish common understanding of this initiative as an inclusive, local chapter program strategy not familiar to the national leadership located in corporate headquarters. CI is a very democratic, less hierarchical model that is in contrast to the ways things normally get done in the organization. One vector for learning was how to better initiate action in this culture. One consequence was coming to expect a slower pace for the inquiry, as a result of having to recognize and develop learning opportunities with corporate stakeholders.

These efforts all point to the need for more experience in implementing collaborative inquiries in different institutional and organizational contexts.

What Are the Advantages and Disadvantages of Having Two or More Initiators?

Learning more about the advantages and disadvantages of co-initiation is another area for future exploration. This may be important in certain institutional contexts as a way of building additional support for the inquiry. On the other hand, having two or more initiators can complicate the process, especially around the direction taken by the inquiry. An issue confronting all initiators is letting go of their sense of ownership as the co-inquiry process evolves. This issue may be more difficult when co-initiators are involved, especially if they see each other frequently outside the inquiry. Depending on the nature of their interaction, they may unintentionally reinforce their sense of ownership. We need more understanding of how to recognize when this and other pitfalls are emerging. There is also a need to learn more about how the other group members perceive co-initiators. Specifically, does it complicate the transition from the initiator role to co-inquirers in terms of the reactions of other group members? How does it influence the building of trust in the group? Additional experience with the co-initiator role is needed to understand more fully the potential issues for contexts.

How Can Collaborative Inquiry Be Conducted at a Distance?

Earlier in this chapter we discussed the role technology can play in helping inquirers overcome the limitations of physical distance. However, we still emphasized the importance face-to-face contact plays in inquiry. However, the issue of distance inquiry, like distance learning, cannot be dismissed out of hand. More experience is needed in this area to determine the viability of conducting collaborative inquiry in a distance mode, exploring the potential and limitations for practice.

CONCLUDING COMMENTS

We hope this book answers many of the questions adult learning practitioners and others may have about collaborative inquiry and invites others to engage in what we know to be an effective adult learning and research strategy and an effective agent of change. The questions raised in this chapter are only the beginning of a long and exciting process; as more people gain experience in collaborative inquiry, more questions will arise.

Collaborative inquiry as a learning and research tool is particularly important in these years of radical change in the workplace, in education, and in societal values. More and more people are creating new work niches in information and delivery systems. The issues and questions arising in this period of change are particularly suited to collaborative inquiry. The only "right" answers are those that help resolve the socioeconomic disequilibrium that challenges our confidence in our values and our society. Collaborative inquiry is inclusive in terms of participation, open in terms of ideas that may be considered.

We continue to find ourselves inexorably drawn to new cycles of action, reflection, and meaning-making about collaborative inquiry. We also anticipate eagerly the learning that comes from others who engage in the process.

Appendix:
Divergent Paths and Visions

We began the journey of writing this book to share our experience with collaborative inquiry in a way that would offer insight into the experience and provide guidance to those interested in initiating their own inquiries. Our initial draft intertwined what one reader described as two focuses: a report of the thINQ inquiries that sought to capture its particular experience and our learning about conducting CI. Reviewers of the first draft suggested that the principal contribution of this book is in bringing clarity to the latter. As our focus became providing a framework for our emerging understanding of collaborative inquiry including both its theoretical foundations, this was not a project for which Annette had energy and she withdrew, wishing us well. The four of us became even more convinced of the need for the direction the project subsequently took, especially as our subsequent experiences with CI in different contexts became part of the basis for our collaborative writing process. For benefit of our readers, Annette's reasons for not pursuing the project, in her own words, are below.

* * *

When I finally decided to pursue a doctorate, it was with a firmly held conviction to find a rigorous and alternative academic program. The Columbia AEGIS program offered a decidedly different approach, and

Elizabeth Kasl's challenge to pursue a doctorate collaboratively provided a perfect fit.

The five members of thINQ worked about as closely as five adults separated by geography and profession could; in fact, for over 3 years, our lives and thought grew more entwined, manifested through common language and tacit understandings.

My decision to withdraw from this book was painful and regrets still linger. But I have been unable to reconcile the contradictions between the lived experience of collaborative inquiry and the academic approach herein. Reason and Rowan (1981a) established clearly, and our own experience confirmed, that collaborative inquiry is a nontraditional model of creating meaning. The revised "traditional academic" structure and tone of this book obscure this basic tenet of collaborative learning. Attempting to fit the lively and evolving form of collaborative inquiry into a traditional presentation requires eliminating the most crucial aspect of the process: its erratic cycles of experience and reflection that, while difficult to represent to the reader, are the core and the life of the experience. By excising this from the text, the excitement and breadth of the experience are reduced and diminished.

I know that what thINQ accomplished is significant and innovative; distorting the experience by fitting it into a traditional academic exposition is a violation of the process and, more important, a disservice to readers hoping to implement collaborative inquiry as a learning tool.

If collaborative inquiry were just another traditional mode of learning, my decision to withdraw might be seen as personal or group failure; it is one of the important strengths of the process that this decision is a manifestation of the process—one that is messy and that has no firm beginning or end.

—Annette Zelman

References

Adler, P., & Adler, P. A. (1987). *Membership roles in field research*. Beverly Hills, CA: Sage.

Argyris, C. (1968). Some unintended consequences of rigorous research. *Psychological Bulletin, 70,* 185-197.

Argyris, C. (1982). *Reasoning, learning, and action: Individual and organizational.* San Francisco: Jossey-Bass.

Argyris, C. (1985). *Strategy, change, and defensive routines.* Boston: Pitman.

Argyris, C. (1996). Actionable knowledge: Design causality in the service of consequential theory. *Journal of Applied Behavioral Science, 32,* 390-406.

Argyris, C., Putnam, R., & Smith, D. M. (1985). *Action science: Concepts, methods, and skills for research and intervention.* San Francisco: Jossey-Bass.

Argyris, C., & Schon, D. A. (1974). *Theory in practice: Increasing interpersonal effectiveness.* San Francisco: Jossey-Bass.

Armstrong, J. L., & Yarbrough, S. L. (1996). Group learning: The role of the environment. In S. Imel (Ed.), *Learning in groups: Exploring fundamental principles, new uses, and emerging opportunities* (New Directions for Adult and Continuing Education, 71, pp. 33-39). San Francisco: Jossey-Bass.

Bion, W. R. (1961). *Experiences in groups, and other papers.* London: Tavistock.

Bohm, D. (1996). In L. Nichol (Ed.), *On dialogue.* New York: Routledge.

Boud, D., Keogh, R., & Walker, D. (1985a). Promoting reflection in learning: A model. In D. Boud, R. Keogh, & D. Walker (Eds.), *Reflection: Turning experience into learning* (pp. 18-40). London: Kogan Page.

Boud, D., Keogh, R., & Walker, D. (1985b). What is reflection in learning? In D. Boud, R. Keogh, & D. Walker (Eds.), *Reflection: Turning experience into learning* (pp. 7-17). London: Kogan Page.

Bray, J. N. (1995). The noetic experience of learning in collaborative inquiry groups: From descriptive, hermeneutic, and eidetic phenomenological perspectives. *Dissertation Abstracts International, 56*(07), 2524. (University Microfilms No. AAC95-39779)

Brooks, A. (1994). Power and the production of knowledge: Collective team learning in work organizations. *Human Resource Development Quarterly, 5,* 213-235.

Brooks, A., & Watkins, K. E. (1994). A new era for action technologies: A look at the issues. In A. Brooks & K. Watkins (Eds.), *The emerging power of action inquiry technologies* (New Directions for Adult and Continuing Education, 43, pp. 5-16). San Francisco: Jossey-Bass.

Brown, L. D. (1993). Participatory action research for social change: Collective reflections with Asian nongovernmental development organizations. *Human Relations, 46,* 249-273.

Burke, W. W. (1982). *Organizational development: Principles and practices.* Boston: Little, Brown.

Cahoon, B. (1996). Group learning and technology. In S. Imel (Ed.), *Learning in groups: Exploring fundamental principles, new uses, and emerging opportunities* (New Directions for Adult and Continuing Education, 71, pp. 61-69). San Francisco: Jossey-Bass.

Candy, P. C. (1991). *Self-direction for lifelong learning: A comprehensive guide to theory and practice.* San Francisco: Jossey-Bass.

Cell, E. (1984). *Learning to learn from experience.* Albany: State University of New York Press.

Cherns, A. B. (1975). Action research. In L. E. Davis & A. B. Cherns (Eds.), *The quality of working life: Vol. 2, Cases and commentary* (pp. 27-32). New York: Free Press.

Clark, A. W. (1976). Introduction. In A. W. Clark (Ed.), *Experimenting with organizational life* (pp. 1-7). New York: Plenum.

Clark, P. A. (1972). *Action research and organizational change.* New York: Harper & Row.

Coles, R. (1989). *The call of stories: Teaching and the moral imagination.* Boston: Houghton Mifflin.

Collins, M. (1991). *Adult education as vocation: A critical role for the adult educator.* New York: Routledge.

Cooperrider, D., & Srivastva, S. (1987). Appreciative inquiry in organizational life. *Research in organizational change and development, 1,* 129-169.

Creswell, J. W. (1998). *Qualitative inquiry and research design: Choosing among five traditions.* Thousand Oaks, CA: Sage.

Culbert, S. (1974). *The organization trap.* New York: Basic Books.

Dechant, K., Marsick, V. J., & Kasl, E. (1993). Towards a Model of Team Learning. *Studies in Continuing Education, 15*(1), 1-14.

Dennis, C., Cederholm, L., & Yorks, L. (1996). Learning your way to a global organization: Grace Cocoa. In K. Watkins & V. J. Marsick (Eds.), *Creating the learning organization* (pp. 165-177). Alexandria, VA: American Society for Training and Development.

Deutsch, M. (1968). Field theory in social psychology. In G. Lindzey & E. Aronson (Eds.), *The handbook of social psychology. Vol. 1* (2nd ed.) (pp. 412-487). Reading, MA: Addison-Wesley.

Dewey, J. (1910). *How we think.* Chicago: University of Chicago Press.

Dyer, W. G., & Wilkins, A. L. (1991). Better stories, not better constructs, to generate theory: A rejoinder to Eisenhardt. *Academy of Management Review, 16,* 613-619.

Eisenhardt, K. M. (1989). Building theories from case study research. *Academy of Management Review, 14,* 532-550.

Eisenhardt, K. M. (1991). Better stories and better constructs: The case for rigor and comparative logic. *Academy of Management Review, 16,* 620-627.

Elden, M. (1981). Sharing the research work: New role demands for participatory researchers. In R. Reason & J. Rowan (Eds.), *Human inquiry: A sourcebook of new paradigm research* (pp. 253-266). New York: John Wiley.

Elden, M., & Chisholm, R. F. (1993). Emerging varieties of action research: Introduction to the special issue. *Human Relations, 46,* 121-141.

Elden, M., & Gjersvik, R. (1994). Democratizing action research at work: A Scandinavian model. In A. Brooks & K. Watkins (Eds.), *The emerging power of action inquiry technologies* (New Directions for Adult and Continuing Education, 43, pp. 31-42). San Francisco: Jossey-Bass.

Elden, M., & Levin, M. (1991). Co-generative learning: Bringing participation into action research. In W. F. Whyte (Ed.), *Participatory action research* (pp.127-142). Newbury Park, CA: Sage.

Elias, J. L., & Merriam, S. (1980). *Philosophical foundations of adult education.* Malabar, FL: Krieger.

Elmes, M. B., & Gemmill, G. (1990). The psychodynamics of mindlessness and dissent in small groups. *Small Group Research, 21,* 28-44.

Emery, F. E. (Ed.). (1969). *Systems thinking.* Harmondsworth, England: Penguin.

Fisher, D., & Torbert, W. R. (1995). *Personal and organizational transformations: The true challenge of continual quality improvement.* London: McGraw-Hill.

Freire, P. (1990). *Pedagogy of the oppressed.* New York: Herder & Herder.

French, W. L., & Bell, C. H. Jr. (1995). *Organizational development: Behavioral science interventions for organizational improvement* (5th ed.). Englewood Cliffs, NJ: Prentice Hall.

Gadamer, H. G. (1987). The problem of historical consciousness (J. F. Close, Trans.). In P. Rabinow & W. M. Sullivan (Eds.), *Interpretive social science: A second look* (pp. 82-140). Berkeley: University of California Press. (Reprinted from *La probleme de la conscience historique.* Louvain: Insitut Superieur de Philosophie, Universite Catholique do Louvain, 1963)

Gadamer, H. G. (1993). *Truth and method* (J. Weinsheimer & D. G. Marshall, Trans.) (2nd, rev. ed.). New York: Continuum.

Gerdau, J. A. (1995). Learning in adulthood through collaborative inquiry. *Dissertation Abstracts International, 56*(07), 25247. (University Microfilms No. AAC95-39807)

Gerdau-Lee, J. A., & Davis, H. (1998). *Report on professional inquiry groups for Goals 2000: Educate America.* Unpublished report. Millburn Township Public Schools. Millburn/Short Hills, NJ.

Group for Collaborative Inquiry. (1991). Democratizing knowledge: A model for collaborative inquiry. In *32nd Annual Adult Education Research Conference Proceedings.* Norman: University of Oklahoma Center for Continuing Education.

Group for Collaborative Inquiry (1993). Democratizing knowledge. *Adult Education Quarterly, 44,* 43-51.

Group for Collaborative Inquiry & thINQ. (1994). Collaborative inquiry for the public arena. In A. Brooks & K. Watkins (Eds.), *The emerging power of action inquiry technologies* (New Directions for Adult and Continuing Education, 43, pp. 57-67). San Francisco: Jossey-Bass.

Guba, E. G., & Lincoln, Y. S. (1981). *Effective evaluation.* San Francisco: Jossey-Bass.

Habermas, J. (1971). *Knowledge and human interests* (J. J. Shapiro, Trans.). Boston: Beacon.

Habermas, J. (1984). *The theory of communicative action. Vol 1: Reason and the rationalization of society. Vol 2: Life-world and system: A critique of functionalist reason* (T. McCarthy, Trans.). Boston: Beacon.

Harman, W. W. (1990). Shifting context for executive behavior: Signs of change and revaluation. In S. Srivastva, D. L. Cooperrider, and Associates (Eds.), *Appreciative management and leadership: The power of positive thought and action in organizations* (pp. 37-54). San Francisco: Jossey-Bass.

Hart, M. (1990). Critical theory and beyond: Further perspectives on emancipatory education. *Adult Education Quarterly, 40,* 125-138.

Heron, J. (1981). Experiential research methodology. In R. Reason & J. Rowan (Eds.), *Human inquiry: A sourcebook of new paradigm research* (pp. 153-166). New York: John Wiley.

Heron, J. (1985). The role of reflection in co-operative inquiry. In D. Boud, R. Keogh, & D. Walker (Eds.), *Reflection: Turning experience into learning* (pp. 128-138). London: Kogan Page.

Heron, J. (1988). Validity in co-operative inquiry. In P. Reason (Ed.), *Human inquiry in action: Developments in new paradigm research* (pp. 40-59). London: Sage.

Heron, J. (1992). *Feeling and personhood: Psychology in another key.* London: Sage.

Heron, J. (1996). *Co-operative inquiry: Research into the human condition.* London: Sage.

Honey, P., & Mumford, A. (1989). *Manual of learning opportunities.* King of Prussia, PA: Organization Design and Development.

Husserl, E. (1960). *Cartesian meditations* (Dorion Cairns, Trans.). The Hague: Nijhoff.

Imel, S. (1996). Summing up: Themes and issues related to learning in groups. In S. Imel (Ed.), *Learning in groups: Exploring fundamental principles, new uses, and emerging opportunities* (New Directions for Adult and Continuing Education, 71, pp. 91-96). San Francisco: Jossey-Bass.

Imel, S., & Tisdell, E. J. (1996). The relationship between theories about groups and adult learning groups. In S. Imel (Ed.), *Learning in groups: Exploring fundamental principles, new uses, and emerging opportunities* (New Directions for Adult and Continuing Education, 71, 15-24). San Francisco: Jossey-Bass.

Intuition Group Transcript, 1993. Reported in Zelman, 1995.

Isaacs, W. N. (1993). Taking flight: Dialogue, collective thinking, and organization learning. *Organization Dynamics, 22*(2), 24-39.

Janis, I. L. (1972). *Victims of groupthink.* Boston: Houghton Mifflin.

Janis, I. L. (1982). *Groupthink* (2nd ed.). Boston: Houghton Mifflin.

Jarvis, P. (1992). *Paradoxes of learning: On becoming an individual in society.* San Francisco: Jossey-Bass.

Jick, T. D. (1979). Mixing qualitative and quantitative methods: Triangulation in action. *Administrative Science Quarterly, 24,* 602-611.

Jorgensen, D. L. (1989). *Participant observation: A methodology for human studies.* Newbury Park, CA: Sage.

Kasl, E., Dechant, K., & Marsick, V. J. (1993). Living the learning: Internalizing our model of group learning. In D. Boud, R. Cohen, & D. Walker (Eds.), *Using experience for learning* (pp. 143-156). Bristol, PA: Society for Research into Higher Education and Open University Press.

Kasl, E., Marsick, V. J., & Dechant, K. (1997). Teams as learners: A research-based model of team learning. *The Journal of Applied Behavioral Science, 33,* 227-246.

Kirk, J., & Miller, M. L. (1986). *Reliability and validity in qualitative research.* Sage University Paper Series on Qualitative Research Methods: Vol 2. Beverly Hills, CA: Sage.

Kolb, D. A. (1984). *Experiential learning.* Englewood Cliffs, NJ: Prentice Hall.

Lewin, K. (1946). Action research and minority problems. *Journal of Social Issues, 2,* 34-36.

Lincoln, Y. (1990). The making of a constructivist: A remembrance of transformations past. In E. Guba (Ed.), *The paradigm dialog* (pp. 67-87). Newbury Park, CA: Sage.

Lincoln, Y., & Guba, E. (1986). But is it rigorous? Trustworthiness and authenticity in naturalistic evaluation. In D. Williams (Ed.), *Naturalistic evaluation*

(New Directions for Program Evaluation, 30, pp. 73-84). San Francisco: Jossey-Bass.

Longley, J., & Pruitt, D. G. (1980). A critique of Janis's theory. *Review of personality and social psychology, 51,* 74-93.

Marsick, V. J., & Cederholm, L. (1988). Developing leadership in international managers—an urgent challenge! *The Columbia Journal of World Business, 23*(4), 3-11.

Marsick, V. J., O'Neil, J., Yorks, L., Nilson, G., & Kolodny, R. (1997). Life on the seesaw: Tensions in Action Reflection Learning. In M. Pedler (Ed.), *Action learning in practice* (3rd ed.) (pp. 339-346). Aldershot, England: Gower.

McDermott, J. J. (Ed.). (1973). *The philosophy of John Dewey: Vol. 1, The structure of experience. Vol. 2, The lived experience.* New York: Putman.

McGill, I., & Beaty, L. (1995). *Action learning: A practitioner's guide.* London: Kogan Page.

McTaggart, R. (1997a). Guiding principles for participatory action research. In R. McTaggart (Ed.), *Participatory action research: International contexts and consequences* (pp. 25-43). Albany: State University of New York Press.

McTaggart, R. (Ed.). (1997b). *Participatory action research: International contexts and consequences.* Albany: State University of New York Press.

Mezirow, J. (1991). *Transformative dimensions of adult learning.* San Francisco: Jossey-Bass.

Mezirow, J. (1995). Transformation theory of adult learning. In M. R. Welton (Ed.), *In defense of the lifeworld* (pp. 39-70). Albany: State University of New York Press.

Miles, M., & Huberman, A. M. (1984). *Qualitative data analysis.* Beverly Hills, CA: Sage.

Miller, N. (1994). Participatory action research: Principles, politics, and possibilities. In A. Brooks & K. Watkins (Eds.), *The emerging power of action inquiry technologies* (New Directions for Adult and Continuing Education, 63, pp. 69-80). San Francisco: Jossey-Bass.

Mirvis, P. H. (1990). Merging of executive heart and mind in crisis management. In S. Srivastva, D. L. Cooperrider, and Associates (Eds.), *Appreciative management and leadership: The power of positive thought and action in organizations* (pp. 55-90). San Francisco: Jossey-Bass.

Mumford, A. (1997). The learning process. In M. Pedler (Ed.), *Action learning in practice* (3rd ed.) (pp. 229-242). Aldershot, England: Gower.

Nisbett, R., & Ross, L. (1980). *Human inference: Strategies and shortcomings of social judgement.* Englewood Cliffs, NJ: Prentice-Hall.

O'Neil, J., & Marsick, V. J. (1994). Becoming critically reflective through action reflection learning.[TM] In A. Brooks & K. Watkins (Eds.), *The emerging power of action inquiry technologies* (New Directions for Adult and Continuing Education, 63, pp. 17-30). San Francisco: Jossey-Bass.

Patton, M. Q. (1990). *Qualitative evaluation and research* (2nd ed.). Newbury Park, CA: Sage.

Pedler, M. (Ed.). (1991). *Action learning in practice* (2nd ed.). Aldershot, England: Gower.

Polkinghorne, D. (1983). *Methodology for the human sciences: Systems of inquiry.* Albany: State University of New York Press.

Polkinghorne, D. (1988). *Narrative knowing and the human sciences.* Albany: State University of New York Press.

Popper, K., & Eccles, J. (1981). *The self and its brain.* Springer-Verlag.

Rapoport, R. N. (1970). Three dilemmas in action research. *Human Relations, 23,* 488-513.

Reason, P. (1988a). The co-operative inquiry group. In P. Reason (Ed.), *Human inquiry in action: Developments in new paradigm research* (pp. 18-39). London: Sage.

Reason, P. (Ed.). (1988b). *Human inquiry in action: Developments in new paradigm research.* London: Sage.

Reason, P. (1998c). Introduction. In P. Reason (Ed.), *Human inquiry in action: Developments in new paradigm research* (pp. 1-17). London: Sage.

Reason, P. (1992). Comments made during meeting with Bray, Lee, Smith, Yorks, and Zelman, at Teachers College, Columbia University, April.

Reason, P. (1994a). Three approaches to participative inquiry. In N. K. Denzin & Y. S. Lincoln (Eds.), *Handbook of qualitative research* (pp. 324-339). Thousand Oaks, CA: Sage.

Reason, P. (Ed.). (1994b). *Participation in human inquiry.* Thousand Oaks, CA: Sage.

Reason, P., & Rowan, J. (Eds.). (1981a). *Human inquiry: A sourcebook of new paradigm research.* New York: John Wiley.

Reason, P., & Rowan, J. (1981b). Issues of validity in new paradigm research. In P. Reason (Ed.), *Human inquiry in action: Developments in new paradigm research* (pp. 239-250). London: Sage.

Revans, R. (1982). *The origin and growth of action learning.* Bickly, England: Chartwell-Bratt.

Richardson, L. (1994). Writing: A method of inquiry. In N. K. Denzin & Y. S. Lincoln (Eds.), *Handbook of Qualitative Research* (pp. 516-529). Newbury Park, CA: Sage.

Ricoeur, P. (1971). The model of the text: Meaningful action considered as a text. *Social Research, 38,* 529-562.

Ricoeur, P. (1974). *The conflict of interpretations.* Evanston, IL: Northwestern University Press.

Ricoeur, P. (1986). *From text to action: Essays in hermeneutics, II* (K. Balamey & J. B. Thompson, Trans.). Evanston, IL: Northwestern University Press.

Rogers, C. R. (1961). *On becoming a person: A therapist's view of psychotherapy.* London: Constable.

Rowan, J. (1981). A dialectical paradigm for research. In R. Reason & J. Rowan (Eds.), *Human inquiry: A sourcebook of new paradigm research* (pp. 93-112). New York: John Wiley.

Schein, E. H. (1993). On dialogue, culture, and organization. *Organization Dynamics, 22(2),* 40-51.

Schon, D. (1983). *The reflective practitioner.* New York: Basic Books.

Schrage, M. (1989). *No more teams! Mastering the dynamics of creative collaboration.* New York: Currency Doubleday.

Schutz, A. (1967). *The phenomenology of the social world.* Evanston, IL: Northwestern University Press.

Seashore, S. E. (1976). The design of action research. In A. W. Clark (Ed.), *Experimenting with organizational life* (pp. 103-117). New York: Plenum.

Smith, L. L. (1995). Collaborative inquiry as an adult learning strategy. *Dissertation Abstracts International, 56*(07), 2533. (University Microfilms No. AAC95-39867)

Sperry, R. (1981). Changing priorities. *Annual Review of Neurosciences, 6,* 1-10.

Srivastva, S., Fry, R. E., & Cooperrider, D. L. (1990). Introduction: The call for executive appreciation. In S. Srivastva, D. L. Cooperrider, and Associates (Eds.), *Appreciative management and leadership: The power of positive thought and action in organizations* (pp. 1-33). San Francisco: Jossey-Bass.

Steier, F. (1991). Research as self-reflexivity, self-reflexivity as social process. In F. Steier (Ed.), *Research and reflexivity* (pp. 1-11). Newbury Park, CA: Sage.

Strauss, A., & Corbin, J. (1990). *Basics of qualitative research: Grounded theory procedures and techniques.* Newbury Park, CA: Sage.

Susman, G., & Evered, R. (1978). An assessment of the scientific merit of action research. *Administrative Science Quarterly, 23,* 582-603.

Tandon, R. (1988). Social transformation and participatory research. *Convergence, 21*(2/3), 5-14.

thINQ. (1991-1993). Transcripts from thINQ collaborative inquiry.

thINQ. (1993). Adult learning through collaborative inquiry. In D. Flannery (Ed.), *Proceedings of the 34th Annual Adult Education Research Conference* (pp. 293-298). University Park, PA: Penn State University.

thINQ. (1994). Phenomenology as an interpretive frame: The evolution of a research method for understanding how learning is experienced in collaborative inquiry. In M. Hyams, J. Armstrong, & E. Anderson (Eds.), *Proceedings of the 35th Annual Adult Education Research Conference* (pp. 354-359). Knoxville: University of Tennessee.

Tisdell, E. (1993). Interlocking systems of power, privilege, and oppression in adult higher education classes. *Adult Education Quarterly, 43,* 203-226.

Torbert, W. R. (1981). Why educational research has been so uneducational: The case for a new model of social science based on collaborative inquiry. In P. Reason (Ed.), *Human inquiry in action: Developments in new paradigm research* (pp. 141-151). London: Sage.

Torbert, W. R. (1987). *Managing the corporate dream: Restructuring for long-term success.* Homewood, IL: Dow Jones-Irwin.

Torbert, W. R. (1991). *The power of balance.* Newbury Park, CA: Sage.

Trist, E. L. (1976). Engaging with large-scale systems. In A. W. Clark (Ed.), *Experimenting with organizational life* (pp. 43-57). New York: Plenum.

van Manen, M. (1990). *Researching lived experience: Human science for an action sensitive pedagogy.* Albany: State University of New York Press.

Welton, M. (1991). Shaking the foundations: The critical turn in adult education. *The Canadian Journal for the Study of Adult Education, 5,* 21-42.

Whyte, W. F. (1991a). Introduction. In W. F. Whyte (Ed.), *Participatory action research* (pp. 7-13). Newbury Park, CA: Sage.

Whyte, W. F. (1991b). *Social theory for action: How individuals and organizations learn to change.* Newbury Park, CA: Sage.

Whyte, W. F. (1992). Note on concept clarification in research methodology. *Collaborative Inquiry, 8,* 5-6.

Yorks, L. (1995). Understanding how collaborative inquiry is experienced through collaborative inquiry. *Dissertation Abstracts International, 56*(07), 2534. (University Microfilms No. AAC95-39884)

Yorks, L., O'Neil, J., & Marsick, V. J. (1999). Action learning: Theoretical bases and varieties of practice. In L. Yorks, J. O'Neil, & V. Marsick (Eds.), *Action learning: Successful strategies for individual, team, and organizational development,* (Advances in Developing Human Resources, 2, pp. 1-18). Baton Rouge, LA: Academy of Human Resource Development, and San Francisco: Berrett-Koehler Communications.

Yorks, L., O'Neil, J., Marsick, V. J., Nilson, G., & Kolodny, R. (1996). Boundary management in Action Reflection Learning™ research: Taking the role of a sophisticated barbarian. *Human Resource Development Quarterly, 7,* 313-329.

Zelman, A. W. (1995). Answering the question, "How is learning experienced in collaborative inquiry?" A phenomenological/hermeneutic approach. *Dissertation Abstracts International, 56*(07), 2534. (University Microfilms No. AAC95-39885)

Index

151

About the Authors

John N. Bray is a secondary science teacher and staff development specialist in northern New York. He has established several collaborative inquiry groups with public school teachers, each of which has researched the improvement of their workplace environment. He has received many teaching honors, including New York State Teacher of the Year 2000 finalist, and national recognition for the use of technology in the classroom. His research interests are in the areas of collaborative inquiry, adult learning, qualitative research methodologies, and educational philosophy. He holds three master's degrees (Syracuse University–Bacteriology and Botany; Potsdam College of the State University of New York–Biology Education; and Teachers College, Columbia University–Adult Education). His doctoral degree in Adult Education is from Teachers College, Columbia University.

Joyce Lee has extensive experience as an educational consultant and staff development specialist, with special expertise in working with teachers to introduce technology into the classroom. She has worked at the state level in New Jersey as a consultant on technology use in the classroom and was instrumental in working with teachers in the Millburn School System to further the effective use of technology for instructional purposes. She has also created online graduate courses in management and organizational learning for Thomas Edison College in New Jersey. Most recently, she has used a collaborative inquiry model to help foster large-system change in the use of classroom technology, utilizing the Internet for group dialogue. She holds a master's degree in Educational Technology and a doctorate in Adult Education, both from Teachers College, Columbia University.

Linda L. Smith is President of Smith Consulting, providing facilitation, coaching, and evaluation services to organizations, boards, and staffs. Based in Washington, D.C., she uses storytelling and collaborative inquiry to make team culture useful for workplace learning. During the past 5 years, her projects have included building partnerships for better child health (New Mexico), helping charter school staff use teams (District of Columbia), and coaching strategic development among visual artists (Alexandria, Virginia). She has developed collaborative evaluation strategies for distance learning projects and cross-cultural programs. She has also researched informal learning among women in other cultures: South Africa, Northern Ireland, and New Zealand. She has earned master's degrees from Teachers College, Columbia University (Adult Education) and the University of Tennessee (Nutrition and Public Health Education), and her doctorate at Teachers College, Columbia University (Adult Education).

Lyle Yorks is Associate Professor in the Department of Organization and Leadership at Teachers College, Columbia University. He also serves on the faculties of EMBA programs at the University of Tennessee and the Executive Education faculty at LSU. He regularly consults with companies worldwide on issues related to organizational change and learning, executive development, and performance management. He is the author of several books and chapters and has authored and coauthored articles in *Academy of Management Review, California Management Review, Human Resource Development Quarterly, Sloan Management Review,* and other scholarly and professional journals. His current research interests center around the use of action learning, collaborative inquiry, and related participative strategies for organizational and social learning. He holds master's degrees from Vanderbilt University (Sociology–Complex Organizations) and Teachers College, Columbia University (Adult Education–Organization Learning), and he earned his doctorate at Columbia Teachers College.

Made in the USA
Lexington, KY
10 October 2012